Step Forward
Language for Everyday Life

Multilevel Activity Book

SERIES DIRECTOR
Jayme Adelson-Goldstein

2 Sandy Wagner

OXFORD
UNIVERSITY PRESS

OXFORD
UNIVERSITY PRESS

198 Madison Avenue
New York, NY 10016 USA

Great Clarendon Street, Oxford OX2 6DP UK

Oxford University Press is a department of the University of Oxford.
It furthers the University's objective of excellence in research, scholarship,
and education by publishing worldwide in

Oxford New York

Auckland Cape Town Dar es Salaam Hong Kong Karachi
Kuala Lumpur Madrid Melbourne Mexico City Nairobi
New Delhi Shanghai Taipei Toronto

With offices in

Argentina Austria Brazil Chile Czech Republic France Greece
Guatemala Hungary Italy Japan Poland Portugal Singapore
South Korea Switzerland Thailand Turkey Ukraine Vietnam

oxford and oxford english are registered trademarks of
Oxford University Press

Executive Publisher: Janet Aitchison
Editorial Manager: Stephanie Karras
Editor: Sharon Sargent
Art Director: Maj-Britt Hagsted
Senior Art Editor: Judi DeSouter
Art Editor: Justine Eun
Production Manager: Shanta Persaud
Production Controller: Zainaltu Jawat Ali

Printed in Hong Kong

10 9 8 7 6 5 4 3 2 1

ISBN-13: 978 0 19 4398251
ISBN-10: 0 19 4398250

Acknowledgements

Illustrations by: Shawn Banner: 19, 28, 39, 59, 79, 99, 119; Kathy Baxendale:
84, 124; Richard Deverell: 29, 49, 69, 89, 109, 129; Greg Harris/Cornell &
McCarthy: 64; Michael Hortens: 53, 93, 123; Rose Lowry: 34, 44, 54, 74,
94, 114; Karen Minot: 23, 83, 103, 133; Susan Spellman/Gwen Walters:
38, 58, 88, 104, 118; Gary Torrisi/Gwen Walters: 18, 24, 48, 68, 78, 98, 108,
128, 134.

We would like to thank the following for their permission to reproduce photographs
Dennis Kitchen Studio: 1.

Many thanks to Stephanie Karras for giving me
the opportunity to author for OUP and to Sharon
Sargent for her support, suggestions, and patience.
Special thanks go to Fayne Johnson and Sarah for
their love and support and my three sons who
are always there in spite of busy schedules and
distance. I dedicate this book to a special group of
devoted educators—ESOL practitioners with the
hopes that these activities will provide a useful,
instructional resource for years to come.
Sandy Wagner

It's with great pleasure that I acknowledge the
Multilevel Activity Book 2 team members, all of
whom performed their assigned roles with panache:
Sandy Wagner—creative yet pragmatic writer;
Sharon Sargent—witty and wise facilitator;
Maj-Britt Hagsted, Judi deSouter and Justine Eun—
artful designers: and Stephanie Karras and Janet
Aitchison—gentle timekeepers and devoted
question askers.
Jayme Adelson-Goldstein

Acknowledgments

The Publisher and Series Director would like to acknowledge the following individuals for their invaluable input during the development of this series:

Vittoria Abbatte-Maghsoudi Mount Diablo Unified School District, Loma Vista Adult Center, Concord, CA

Karen Abell Durham Technical Community College, Durham, NC

Millicent Alexander Los Angeles Unified School District, Huntington Park-Bell Community Adult School, Los Angeles, CA

Diana Allen Oakton Community College, Skokie, IL

Bethany Bandera Arlington Education and Employment Program, Arlington, VA

Sandra Bergman New York City Department of Education, New York, NY

Chan Bostwick Los Angeles Technology Center, Los Angeles, CA

Diana Brady-Herndon Napa Valley Adult School, Napa, CA

Susan Burlos Baldwin Park Unified School District, Baldwin Park, CA

Carmen Carbajal Mitchell Community College, Statesville, NC

Jose Carmona Daytona Beach Community College, Daytona Beach, FL

Ingrid Caswell Los Angeles Technology Center, Los Angeles, CA

Joyce Clapp Hayward Adult School, Hayward, CA

Beverly deNicola Capistrano Unified School District, San Juan Capistrano, CA

Edward Ende Miami Springs Adult Center, Miami Springs, FL

Gayle Fagan Harris County Department of Education, Houston, TX

Richard Firsten Lindsey Hopkins Technical Education Center, Miami, FL

Elizabeth Fitzgerald Hialeah Adult Center, Hialeah, FL

Mary Ann Florez Arlington Education and Employment Program, Arlington, VA

Leslie Foster Davidson Mitchell Community College, Statesville, NC

Beverly Gandall Santa Ana College School of Continuing Education, Santa Ana, CA

Rodriguez Garner Westchester Community College, Valhalla, NY

Sally Gearhart Santa Rosa Junior College, Santa Rosa, CA

Norma Guzman Baldwin Park Unified School District, Baldwin Park, CA

Lori Howard UC Berkeley, Education Extension, Berkeley, CA

Phillip L. Johnson Santa Ana College Centennial Education Center, Santa Ana, CA

Kelley Keith Mount Diablo Unified School District, Loma Vista Adult Center, Concord, CA

Blanche Kellawon Bronx Community College, Bronx, NY

Keiko Kimura Triton College, River Grove, IL

Jody Kirkwood ABC Adult School, Cerritos, CA

Matthew Kogan Evans Community Adult School, Los Angeles, CA

Laurel Leonard Napa Valley Adult School, Napa, CA

Barbara Linek Illinois Migrant Education Council, Plainfield, IL

Alice Macondray Neighborhood Centers Adult School, Oakland, CA

Ronna Magy Los Angeles Unified School District Central Office, Los Angeles, CA

Jose Marlasca South Area Adult Education, Melbourne, FL

Laura Martin Adult Learning Resource Center, Des Plaines, IL

Judith Martin-Hall Indian River Community College, Fort Pierce, FL

Michael Mason Mount Diablo Unified School District, Loma Vista Adult Center, Concord, CA

Katherine McCaffery Brewster Technical Center, Tampa, FL

Cathleen McCargo Arlington Education and Employment Program, Arlington, VA

Todd McDonald Hillsborough County Public Schools, Tampa, FL

Rita McSorley Northeast Independent School District, San Antonio, TX

Gloria Melendrez Evans Community Adult School, Los Angeles, CA

Vicki Moore El Monte-Rosemead Adult School, El Monte, CA

Meg Morris Mountain View Los Altos Adult Education District, Los Altos, CA

Nieves Novoa LaGuardia Community College, Long Island City, NY

Jo Pamment Haslett Public Schools, East Lansing, MI

Liliana Quijada-Black Irvington Learning Center, Houston, TX

Ellen Quish LaGuardia Community College, Long Island City, NY

Mary Ray Fairfax County Public Schools, Springfield, VA

Tatiana Roganova Hayward Adult School, Hayward, CA

Nancy Rogenscky-Roda Hialeah-Miami Lakes Adult Education and Community Center, Hialeah, FL

Lorraine Romero Houston Community College, Houston, TX

Edilyn Samways The English Center, Miami, FL

Kathy Santopietro Weddel Northern Colorado Literacy Program, Littleton, CO

Dr. G. Santos The English Center, Miami, FL

Fran Schnall City College of New York Literacy Program, New York, NY

Mary Segovia El Monte-Rosemead Adult School, El Monte, CA

Edith Smith City College of San Francisco, San Francisco, CA

Alisa Takeuchi Chapman Education Center Garden Grove, CA

Leslie Weaver Fairfax County Public Schools, Falls Church, VA

David Wexler Napa Valley Adult School, Napa, CA

Bartley P. Wilson Northeast Independent School District, San Antonio, TX

Emily Wonson Hunter College, New York, NY

Contents

Unit 5 On the Job

Unit 6 Pick Up the Phone

Unit 7 What's for Dinner?

Unit 8 Stay Safe and Well

Unit 9 Money Matters

Unit 10 Steps to Citizenship

Unit 11 Deal with Difficulties

Unit 12 Take the Day Off

Introduction to the *Step Forward Multilevel Activity Book 2*

Welcome to the *Step Forward Multilevel Activity Book 2*. In these pages you'll find a wealth of highly interactive activities that require little preparation. All of the activities can be used in numerous ways with a variety of learners. The 110 activities in this book are effective in high-beginning classes as well as in multilevel classes with learners ranging from newcomers to low-intermediate levels.

This book is divided into 12 units that directly correspond to *Step Forward Student Book 2*. Each activity supports and expands upon the student book's lesson objectives, for a complete approach to English language learning.

1 What is the Multilevel Activity Book?

The *Multilevel Activity Book 2* (like the entire *Step Forward* series) is based on research that says adults taught in a learner-centered classroom retain more material for longer periods of time (McCombs and Whistler, 1997; Benson and Voller, 1997). Through its guided and communicative practice opportunities, the *Multilevel Activity Book 2* provides hours of meaningful and fun classroom activities.

2 How do I use these reproducible activities?

The Teaching Notes on pages 3–13 give detailed directions on how to conduct each activity. They also provide multilevel suggestions, guiding you through

1. setting up the activity,
2. modeling/demonstrating the activity, and
3. checking your learners' comprehension of each activity's goal and directions.

Once learners understand how to proceed, they are able to work together to complete the activities. Putting learning into the learners' hands is an important step towards ensuring that they will achieve the lesson objective. Moving away from the front-and-center role frees you to circulate, monitor, facilitate, and gain insight into how well the lesson information was captured. You discover what learners can and can't do well, and adjust your future lesson plans accordingly.

3 What makes these activities multilevel?

One of the key techniques in multilevel instruction is to use materials that can work

The Grid Game in *Multilevel Activity Book 2* allows learners to work at their own level and pace. Higher-level pairs use more complex language to give directions while lower-level pairs use simpler language to perform the same task.

across levels. There are eight activity types in this book. Each one allows you to tailor practice to the learner's abilities, but still have the entire class working on the same basic activity. (See the photo on page one for an example.) Having only ten activity types means that students quickly

understand how to do the activities, requiring less teacher intervention and more learner-directed practice. Each activity includes a Keep Going suggestion for a follow-up activity, such as graphing results, discussing answers, or reporting on a task. The ten activity types are described below.

ACTIVITY	GROUPING STRATEGY	DESCRIPTION	CORRELATION TO *Step Forward Student Book 2*
Mixer	Whole Class	Learners get acquainted as they ask and answer questions.	**Pre-Unit: The First Step**
Round Table Label	Small Groups	Learners take turns labeling unit vocabulary in a scene.	**Lesson 1: Vocabulary**
Vocabulary in Action	Pairs	Learners reinforce their understanding of target words and phrases through Total Physical Response.	**Lesson 2: Life stories**
Peer Dictation	Pairs	Partners take turns dictating sentences that reinforce grammar structures while developing their clarification strategies.	**Lesson 3: Grammar**
Role-Play	Small Groups	Learners develop fluency by practicing and expanding upon conversation gambits.	**Lesson 4: Everyday conversation**
Survey	Whole Class	Learners gather classmates' information and graph the results.	**Lesson 5: Real-life reading**
Team Project	Small Groups	Learners work together to complete a project.	**Review and expand**
Picture Cards	Pairs	Partners use flash cards to study the unit's target vocabulary.	**Review and expand**
Grid Game	Pairs	Partners tell each other where to place picture cards on their grids to end up with matching grids.	**Review and expand**
Sentence Maker	Small Groups	Learners use word cards to make as many statements and questions as they can in ten minutes.	**Review and expand**

By having pairs or small groups practice the language required to meet a lesson objective, teachers facilitate learners' use and internalization of the target language. This also provides important opportunities for learners to engage in real-life interaction strategies such as negotiating meaning, checking information, disagreeing, and reaching consensus.

While a pair of running shoes is not required equipment, most multilevel instructors find

themselves on the move in the classroom. These highly structured activities support the energetic, communicative, and lively approach to learning that is the hallmark of effective multilevel instruction. The Step Forward Team hopes that you and your learners enjoy these activities.

Please write to us with your comments and questions: **Stepforwardteam.us@oup.com.**

Multilevel Activity Teaching Notes

Teaching Notes for the Mixer

Focus: Students get to know each other by asking and answering questions.
Grouping Strategy: Whole class
Activity Time: 25–30 minutes
Student Book Connection: The First Step

Ready,

1. Select a Mixer activity.

2. Duplicate one activity page for each student.

3. Write the first Mixer question/ command on the board.

Set . . .

1. Share the goal of the activity: *You're going to talk to your classmates to learn more about each other.*

2. Have a higher-level volunteer ask you the Mixer question/say the command from the board. Give your answer and then ask the student for his/her answer to the same question.

3. Ask the question/say the command from the board and elicit responses from the class.

4. Distribute an activity page to each student and review the directions.

5. Ask two volunteers to come to the front and model the activity.

6. Check students' comprehension by asking *yes/no* questions. *Do you answer the questions yourself?* [no] *Do you write your name in the chart?* [no]

Go!

1. Set a time limit (five minutes).

2. Have students circulate to complete the activity page. Tell them to sit down when their activity page is complete.

3. Enter the mixer yourself. Students will enjoy your participation and you can check their accuracy.

4. Give students a two-minute warning.

5. Call "time."

Keep Going!

Talk about the results of the mixer using the prompt.

Multilevel Suggestions

Before the Activity:
Pre-Level: Help students read the questions and write their own answers in their notebooks.
On-Level: Have students read the question(s) and write their answers in their notebooks.
Higher-Level: Pair students and have them write three to five new questions on the Mixer topic to add to their activity page.

During the Activity:
On- and higher-level students can stay "in the mix" and help others once their own activity page is complete.

Teaching Notes for the Round Table Label

Focus: Students take turns identifying and labeling the vocabulary depicted in a scene.
Grouping Strategy: Groups of 3–5 students
Activity Time: 20–25 minutes
Student Book Connection: Lesson 1

Ready,

1. Select the Round Table Label activity that corresponds to the unit you are teaching in *Step Forward Student Book 2*.

2. Duplicate one activity page for each group.

3. On the board, post three pictures or draw three objects related to the lesson topic. Draw a line next to each picture. (Students will write the name of the object on the blank line.)

Set . . .

1. Share the goal of the activity: *You're going to work together to label a picture.*

2. Form groups of three to five students.

3. Model the activity. Have one group come forward and take turns passing the chalk and labeling the pictures. Point out that students can label any picture on the board.

4. Once all the pictures are labeled, have the class check the students' spelling in *The Oxford Picture Dictionary* or another dictionary.

5. Distribute one activity page to each group and review the directions.

6. To reinforce the circulation of the activity page within the group, have group members first pass their activity page from student to student, writing their names at the top of the page.

7. Check students' comprehension by asking *yes/no* questions. *Does one person write all the words on the paper?* [no] *Do you pass the paper to the person next to you?* [yes]

Go!

1. Set a time limit (ten minutes). Tell students not to worry about spelling for now. They will check their spelling later.

2. Each student labels one vocabulary item and then passes the sheet to another group member. Students continue taking turns until they've labeled all the items they know.

3. Monitor progress and encourage students to ask their group members for help if they are unsure of a word or its spelling.

4. Call "time" and have students check the spelling of each word in *The Oxford Picture Dictionary* or another dictionary.

Keep Going!

Have students talk about the topic using the discussion prompt on the activity page.

Multilevel Suggestions

For Mixed-Level Groups:
Tell pre-level students that they can say rather than write the words. Instruct on-level and higher-level students to write their pre-level group members' ideas on the activity page.

For Same-Level Groups:
Pre-Level: Give each group of students a list of the words matching the blanks in the picture. Have them complete the activity as outlined above, using the wordlist for help as needed.

On-Level: Have students complete the activity as outlined above.

Higher-Level: Place the picture in the middle of the group and have students pass around a sheet of notebook paper. Have them take turns writing sentences about the picture.

Teaching Notes for Vocabulary in Action

Focus: Students match actions to pictures. Partners then take turns saying and acting out the sentences.
Grouping Strategy: Pairs
Activity Time: 20–30 minutes
Student Book Connection: Lesson 2

Ready,

1. Select the Vocabulary in Action activity that corresponds to the unit you are teaching in *Step Forward Student Book 2.*

2. Duplicate one activity page for each pair.

3. Write out two actions on the right side of the board and illustrate them on the left side of the board. For example, write *Sit down.* and *Stand up.* Draw two stick people: one standing and the other sitting. Number the pictures *1* and *2*.

4. Elicit from students which picture matches which action.

5. Say and demonstrate both actions. Then say the sentences and have students do the actions. Finally, have volunteers say a sentence and you act it out.

Set . . .

1. Share the goal of the activity: *First, you're going to work with a partner and match the pictures and sentences on this page. Then you're going to practice saying the sentences and acting them out.*

2. Pair students and distribute one activity page per pair. Use the example on the page to demonstrate how to do the matching activity.

3. Set a time limit (three minutes) for partners to match the pictures and sentences.

4. Call "time" and check students' accuracy.

5. Have two volunteers demonstrate the next part of the activity.
- Identify one student as Partner A and the other student as Partner B.
- Give Partner A the activity page and direct him/her to say the sentences to Partner B.
- Have Partner B act out the sentences.
- Have Partner B take the activity sheet and say the sentences to Partner A, who acts them out.

6. Check comprehension by asking *yes/no* questions. *Do you show your partner the paper?* [no] *Can you show your partner what to do?* [yes]

Go!

1. Assign A/B roles to pairs and review the directions.

2. Direct Partner B to act out the sentences Partner A says. Set a time limit (five minutes).

3. Call "time" and have students switch roles. Set a time limit (five minutes).

4. Call "time" and have students take turns giving you the commands. Make mistakes so that they have to correct you.

Keep Going!

Put the pairs into groups. Have a student select a sentence and act it out for the group. The rest of the group guesses which sentence the student is acting out. The first student to guess correctly chooses a new sentence and acts it out for the group.

Multilevel Suggestions

For Mixed-Level Pairs:
Pair higher-level or on-level students with pre-level students. Assign the "acting" role to pre-level students.

For Same-Level Pairs:
Pre-Level: Give each student a copy of the activity page and work with these students as a group to present and practice the commands.
On-Level: Have students complete the activity as outlined above.
Higher-Level: Have students work in groups of three. Assign A, B, and C roles. Have Student A give the command, Student B act out the command, and Student C ask Student A a question such as What is he/she doing? or ask Student B *What are you doing?*

Teaching Notes for Peer Dictation

Focus: Students dictate sentences to each other and ask clarification questions to complete the activity page.
Grouping Strategy: Pairs
Activity Time: 15–25 minutes
Student Book Connection: Lesson 3

Ready,

1. Select the Peer Dictation activity that corresponds to the unit you are teaching in *Step Forward Student Book 2*.

2. Duplicate one activity page for each student.

3. On the left side of the board, write a sentence that relates to the topic. Label this side of the board *Partner A*. Label the right side of the board *Partner B*.

4. Familiarize students with the dictation process by asking a volunteer to read the sentence on the left side of the board to you. As you write the sentence on the right side of the board, model one or more clarification strategies: *Can you spell that please?* or *Can you repeat that?*, etc.

Set . . .

1. Share the goal of the activity: *You're going to practice reading, listening to, and writing sentences.*

2. Distribute one activity page per person and review the directions.

3. Pair students. Assign A/B roles to each pair and have them fold their activity pages.

4. Have one volunteer pair model the activity for the class. Ask the pair to come to the front and sit across from each other. Give each partner one of the activity pages. Tell the partners what to do as the class watches and listens.
  • *Fold your papers.*
  • *Partner A, look at the top. Partner B, look at the bottom.*
  • *Partner A, read the first sentence on the page to your partner.*
  • *Partner B, check what you hear.*
  • *Partner B, write the sentence.*

5. When A finishes, have B dictate the first sentence on the bottom half of the sheet to A.

6. Check comprehension by asking *or* questions. *Do you fold or cut the paper?* [fold] *Does Partner A read the A sentences or the B sentences?* [the A sentences]

Go!

1. Set a time limit (five minutes) for A to dictate to B.

2. Call "time" and set a time limit (five minutes) for B to dictate to A.

3. Call "time" and have pairs unfold their papers and check their work.

Keep Going!

Have pairs create four new sentences on the same topic as the Peer Dictation. Have each pair read one of their sentences to the class.

Multilevel Suggestions

For Mixed-Level Pairs:
Pair on-level or higher-level students with pre-level students. Allow pre-level students to either write or to dictate, depending on what they would rather do.

For Same-Level Pairs

Pre-Level: Provide a simplified version of the peer dictation by whiting out all but a key word or phrase on the activity page and then duplicating it for the students. Conduct the activity as outlined above.

On-Level: Have students complete the activity as outlined above.

Higher-Level: Review the information question words: *who, what, where, when.* Direct students to purposely obscure one of the words in each sentence as they dictate, forcing their partner to clarify before they write. For example, Partner A: *Charles is [cough] ing.* Partner B: *What is Charles doing?*

Teaching Notes for the Role-Play

Focus: Working in groups, students read, choose roles, write the ending, and act out a role-play.
Grouping Strategy: Groups of 3–4 students
Activity Time: 60 minutes
Student Book Connection: Lesson 4

Ready,

1. Select the Role-Play activity that corresponds to the unit you are teaching in *Step Forward Student Book 2*.

2. Duplicate one activity page for each student.

3. Check the "Props" list to determine what items you need to bring to class. Each group will need its own set of props.

4. Check the script to determine what, if any, new vocabulary students will need in order to do the role-play.

Set . . .

1. Share the goal of the activity: *You're going to work in groups and act out different parts in a role-play.*

2. Have students form groups according to the number of characters.

3. Distribute one activity page per person and one set of props per group. Review the directions: *First read the script. Next decide who will play each character. Then write an ending. You must add lines for each character.*

4. Present new vocabulary or review vocabulary as needed.

5. Check comprehension by asking yes/no questions. *Do you say all the lines?* [no] *Do you act out your lines?* [yes]

6. Invite two volunteers to the front. Have each pick a line of dialog from the script and act it out for the class.

Go!

1. Set a time limit (ten minutes) for the group to read the script, choose their characters, and finish the role-play.

2. Set a time limit (five minutes), and have the students act out the role-play in their groups.

2. Monitor student progress by walking around and helping with problems such as register or pronunciation (rhythm, stress, and intonation). Encourage pantomime and improvisation.

Keep Going!

Have each group perform their role-play for the class. Ask students, while watching the role-plays, to write the answers to the questions provided in the Keep Going section on the activity page.

Multilevel Suggestions

For Mixed-Level Groups:
Adapt the role-play to include a non-speaking or limited speaking role for pre-level students who are not ready to participate verbally. For example, add a character who only answers *yes* or *no* to questions asked by another character. In larger classes, you may want to assign a higher-level student as a "director" for each group.

For Same-Level Groups:
Pre-Level: On the board, write a simplified conversation based on the role-play situation. Help students read and copy the conversation in their notebooks. Then have pairs practice the conversation until they can perform it without the script.

On-Level: Have students complete the activity as outlined above.

Higher-Level: Have students expand the script to create their own version of the role-play using related vocabulary or a similar situation.

Teaching Notes for the Survey

Focus: Students ask and answer classmates' questions and then work individually to record and graph the results.
Grouping Strategy: Individual
Activity Time: 35 minutes
Student Book Connection: Lesson 5

Ready,

1. Select the Survey activity that corresponds to the unit you're teaching in *Step Forward Student Book 2*.

2. Duplicate one activity page for each student.

3. Write the survey question on the board. Draw a simplified chart on the board based on the first row of the survey chart. Then draw a limited bar graph based on the bar graph in the activity.

4. Ask the first survey question and answer it yourself. Chart your response with a check.

5. Ask four students the same question, checking off their responses on the chart as they answer.

6. Remind students that a bar graph is another way to look at information. Transfer the information from the chart onto the bar graph.

Set . . .

1. Share the goal of the activity: *You're going to ask and answer questions about _____ with your classmates. Then you're going to make a bar graph with the information you learn.*

2. Distribute the activity page and review the directions. Check comprehension by asking information questions. *How many questions do you answer?* [all] *How many people do you talk to?* [nine]

3. Have students silently read and respond to the survey questions, marking their response in the column titled "My Answers."

4. Set a time limit (ten minutes).

Go!

1. Direct students to interview nine other students and mark their responses in the chart.

2. Circulate and monitor.

3. Call "time" and have students return to their seats. Ask volunteers to share the responses on their surveys.

4. Remind students how to fill in the bar graphs on their activity page. Set a time limit (five to ten minutes) and ask them to transfer their survey information to the bar graph.

5. Monitor students' progress, making sure that students' bar graphs match the numbers on their chart.

6. Elicit the results of various students' surveys and write the results on the board in sentence form.

Keep Going!

Have students write five sentences about the results of their survey using the sentences on the board as models.

Multilevel Suggestions

During the Survey:
Pair pre-level students with on- and higher-level students. Have the partners work together to survey nine other pairs.

During the Graphing:
Pre-Level: Work with the pre-level group, helping them make a bar graph showing all their survey results.
On-Level and Higher-Level: Have students complete the bar graph as outlined above.

Teaching Notes for the Team Project

Focus: Students work in a group to complete a project-based learning exercise.
Grouping Strategy: Groups of 4–5 students
Activity Time: 60 minutes
Student Book Connection: Review and Expand

Ready,

1. Select the Team Project that corresponds to the unit you're teaching in *Step Forward Student Book 2.*

2. Duplicate one copy of the activity page for each student.

3. Check the materials needed for the project and gather enough for each group.

4. If possible, create a sample of the project students will be doing (e.g., a poster or newsletter).

5. Provide a review of the vocabulary and concepts students will need to complete the project.

Set . . .

1. Share the goal of the activity: *You're going to work in groups to create* [product]. If you have created a sample of what they'll be producing, show it to the students and answer any questions about it.

2. Have students form groups of four or five. Explain the jobs for the activity (see the individual activity page). Allow students to choose their jobs.

3. Ask the Supplier to pick up activity pages for his/her group.

4. Ask the Group Leaders to read the directions to their groups.

5. Check comprehension by asking *yes/no* questions. *Does one person do all the work?* [no] *Do you make a list of ideas?* [yes]

6. Set a time limit (three to five minutes) for groups to brainstorm answers to the question. The Recorder writes the groups ideas while the Timekeeper watches the clock for the group.

Go!

1. Have students begin to create their projects. Tell students they will have 25–30 minutes to complete their project.

2. Circulate to check students' progress.

3. About twenty minutes into the time period, check with groups to see if they need more time. Extend the time limit by five or ten minutes as needed.

4. Call "time." Have the Reporter from each group tell the class about their project.

Keep Going!

Have students complete the Keep Going activity on the Team Project activity page.

Multilevel Suggestions

For Mixed-Level Groups:
Assign the role of Supplier and Timekeeper to pre-level students. Ask higher-level students to be Group Leaders and Recorders.

For Same-Level Groups:
Pre-Level: Simplify the project by reducing the amount of reading and writing required. For example, with poster projects, have students label items on posters with single words.

On-Level: Have groups complete the project as outlined above.

Higher-Level: Increase the challenge for students by requiring more writing for the project. For example, have students write a paragraph on how well their group worked together.

Teaching Notes for the Picture Cards

Focus: Students review key vocabulary and grammar using picture cards for Flash Cards.
Grouping Strategy: Pairs
Activity Time: Various
Student Book Connection: Review and Expand

Ready,

1. Select the Picture Cards that correspond to the unit you're teaching in *Step Forward Student Book 2*.

2. Duplicate one page of Picture Cards for each pair. Have scissors on hand for each pair.

3. Cut apart one of the Picture Card pages to use in the demonstration.

Set . . .

1. Review the directions and the picture card vocabulary as needed.

2. Pair students.

3. Have pairs cut apart the picture cards and write the corresponding word from the word list on the reverse side of each card.

4. Model the activity for the class. Ask a volunteer to hold up a picture card. Say the corresponding word or phrase. Tell the volunteer to look at the back of the card to check if you are correct. Change roles.

5. Share the goal of the activity: *You will use flash cards to practice vocabulary.*

Go!

1. Assign A/B roles.

2. Partner A holds up a picture card. Partner B says the corresponding vocabulary word or phrase. Partner A looks at the reverse side of the card to verify accuracy. Then the students change roles.

3. Allow students to keep their cards for future use.

Keep Going!

Have pairs form groups of four and take turns using the flash cards to see who can name the most words in the shortest time.

Multilevel Suggestions

For Mixed-Level Pairs or Groups:
Be sure each pair or group has at least one on-level or higher-level student who can help guide the pre-level student(s) through the activity.

For Same-Level Pairs or Groups:
Pre-Level: Work with these students separately to review all the pictures. Have students point to or hold up the pictures as first you, then volunteers, say the word or describe the picture.

On-Level: Have students complete the activities as outlined above.

Higher-Level: Allow groups to create their own games with the picture cards. Have a Recorder write the rules. Ask a Reporter from each group to teach the game to the class.

Teaching Notes for the Grid Game

Focus: Students ask and answer questions in order to create matching picture grids.
Grouping Strategy: Pairs
Activity Time: 30 minutes
Student Book Connection: Review and Expand

Ready,

1. Select the Grid Game and Picture Cards that correspond to the unit you are teaching in *Step Forward Student Book 2*.

2. Duplicate one Picture Card page and one Grid Game page for each student and one for you. Have scissors for each pair. Cut apart one of the Picture Card pages to use in the demonstration.

3. Copy the first row of the activity page grid onto the board.

4. Choose three picture cards and draw simplified versions of these cards on three sheets of paper. Put a piece of tape on each paper so they can be attached to the board.

5. Share the goal of the activity: *You're going to play a game to help you practice vocabulary.*

6. Pair students and give each partner a Grid Game page and a Picture Card page. Have students cut apart their picture cards and place them faceup next to their grid. If possible, give each pair a folder to use as a screen between partners. (See the photo on page 1 as an example.)

Set . . .

1. Ask a volunteer to be your partner. Show your grid page, and tell the student that the grid on the board is his/her "paper." Emphasize you can not look at each other's "papers." Show the class your three picture cards and give your partner the corresponding hand-drawn pictures.

2. Model the activity.
  • Put one picture card on your grid and show the class, but don't show your partner. Then tell your partner where to put the picture card on his/her grid. (If you put the picture of a shirt on the grid square with $30.99 on it, then tell your partner: *The shirt is $30.99.*)
  • Encourage the student to clarify. (Student: *$13. 99 or $30.99?* You: *$30.99.*)
  • Have your partner tape the correct hand-drawn picture onto the board grid. (The student should tape the hand-drawn shirt picture onto the board in the grid square that says $30.99.) Ask: *Are our papers the same?*

3. Model the activity with the entire class. Circulate and check grids. Then change roles. Have the students tell you where to place your picture cards.

Go!

1. Assign A/B roles to each pair. Remind students not to look at each other's grids.

2. Tell the A students they will start by putting a picture on the grid and telling their partners where to put the same picture on their grids.

3. Set a time limit (ten minutes) and have students work until all the picture cards are on the grids.

4. Have the students compare their grids to see how well they communicated.

5. Have the students switch roles. Set another time limit (ten minutes) and play again.

Keep Going!

Have students write five sentences using the Picture Card and Grid Game vocabulary.

Multilevel Suggestions

For Mixed-Level Pairs:
Assign higher-level students the A role, so that they speak first. Whenever possible, pair students who speak different languages.

For Same-Level Pairs:
Pre-Level: Simplify the grid page by giving each square a number. Have partners give the number of the grid square and the vocabulary word. (Partner A: *One— shirt.* Partner B: *Shirt?* Partner A: *Yes.*)

On-Level: Have pairs complete the activity as outlined above.

Higher-Level: Write a more complex dialog on the board and model it for students to use during the game.
A: *Are you looking for a shirt?* B: *Yes, I am.* A: *Here's one for $30.99.* B: *Did you say $13.99?* A: *No, $30.99.* B: *Thanks.*

Teaching Notes for the Sentence Maker

Focus: Students work in small groups to make ten different sentences or questions using word cards.
Grouping Strategy: Groups of 3-4 students
Activity Time: 15-20 minutes
Student Book Connection: Review and Expand

Ready,

1. Select the Sentence Maker activity that corresponds to the unit you're teaching in *Step Forward Student Book 2*.

2. Duplicate one activity page for each group. Have scissors on hand for each group.

3. Draw these six sample "cards" on the board:

CHINA	HE	IS
FROM	?	.

Set . . .

1. Share the goal of the activity: *You're going to work together to make sentences and questions using word cards.*

2. Point out the punctuation cards. Elicit a sentence and a question using the sample cards on the board. Write each on the board.

3. Explain the activity.
- *The group works with the cards to make a sentence or a question.*
- *They dictate the sentence or question to the group's Recorder.*
- *The Recorder writes the sentence and reads it to the group. Then the group repeats the process, making additional sentences and questions.*

4. Check comprehension by asking *yes/no* questions. *Do you write on the cards?* [no] *Do you make more than one sentence?* [yes]

5. Distribute one set of cards and a pair of scissors to each group and review the directions.

6. Have each group cut apart the word cards.

Go!

1. Form groups of three or four and have each group choose a Recorder.

2. Set a time limit (ten minutes) and have groups begin the activity.

3. Monitor and facilitate the students' group work.

4. Call "time." Ask Recorders to tell the number of items they wrote.

Keep Going!

Have each group write two to three of their sentences or questions on the board. Ask the class to give feedback on the accuracy of the sentences.

Multilevel Suggestions

For Mixed-Level Groups:
Create groups that have at least one higher-level student who can serve as the Recorder.

For Same-Level Groups:
Pre-Level: Give pairs a list of sentences and questions that can be made from the cards. Have partners assemble matching sentences with the cards, checking off each sentence on the list as they make it.

On-Level: Have students complete the activity as outlined above.

Higher-Level: Have pairs look at their list of ten sentences/questions they created and write an original corresponding question or sentence for each one.

The First Step

Mixer

What Can You Do?

1. Walk around the room. Ask and answer the questions.

2. Check the box. Write the name.

1. Can you say the days of the week? Do it.

☐ yes _____
(name)

☐ no _____
(name)

2. Can you say the months of the year? Do it.

☐ yes _____
(name)

☐ no _____
(name)

3. Can you say the months that have 30 days? Do it.

☐ yes _____
(name)

☐ no _____
(name)

4. Can you count by ordinal numbers (*first, second, third, . . .*)? Do it.

☐ yes _____
(name)

☐ no _____
(name)

5. Can you say the letters of the alphabet from A to Z? Do it.

☐ yes _____
(name)

☐ no _____
(name)

6. Can you say the letters of the alphabet from Z to A? Do it.

☐ yes _____
(name)

☐ no _____
(name)

KEEP GOING!

Talk about your classmates. How many students can say the alphabet from Z to A?

It's Your Birthday!

1. Walk around the room.

2. Ask your classmates: *When is your birthday?*

3. Write your classmates' name next to their birthday month.

When is your birthday?

	Classmates' Names
January	
February	
March	
April	
May	
June	
July	
August	
September	
October	
November	
December	

KEEP GOING!

Which month has the most birthdays?

Unit 1 Learning to Learn

How Do You Learn?

1. Work with 3 classmates.

2. Label the actions you see in the picture.

3. Check your spelling in a dictionary.

> **KEEP GOING!**
> Talk about how you learn new words. What are your favorite ways to learn?

Learning My Way

1. Work with a partner. Look at the pictures. Match the sentences to the pictures.

2. **Partner A:** Say the sentences.

  Partner B: Act out the sentences. Use actions and words.

3. Change roles.

____ Speak English with classmates.

____ Draw pictures of words.

____ Watch a movie.

____ Go on the Internet.

____ Write sentences.

1 Listen to the teacher.

____ Read books.

____ Put on your headphones. Listen to CDs.

KEEP GOING!
Work in a group. Take turns. Act out the sentences. Say what your classmate is doing.

Unit 1 Vocabulary in Action   **19**

What Do Barbara and Linda Like to Do?

Partner A
• **Read a sentence to Partner B.** • **Answer Partner B's question.** • **Watch Partner B write.**
1. Barbara doesn't want to be alone. 2. She wants to practice English. 3. She likes to talk. 4. She needs to call some friends.
• **Listen to Partner B.** • **Check what you hear. Ask:** *Can you repeat that?* • **Write the sentence.**
5.
6.
7.
8.

- FOLD HERE -

Partner B
• **Listen to Partner A.** • **Check what you hear. Ask:** *Can you repeat that?* • **Write the sentence.**
1.
2.
3.
4.
• **Read a sentence to Partner A.** • **Answer Partner A's question.** • **Watch Partner A write.**
5. Linda wants to be alone. 6. She wants to listen to CDs. 7. She likes to read stories. 8. She doesn't need to talk.

KEEP GOING!

Write 4 sentences about what you like to do alone. Talk about your sentences with your class.
I like to go on the Internet.

Nice to Meet You

1. Work with 3 classmates. Say all the lines in the script.

2. Choose your character.

3. Finish the conversation. Write more lines for each character.

4. Practice the lines.

5. Act out the role-play with your group.

Scene	Characters	Props
A coffee shop	• Charlie • Brenda • Rita • Ned, a coffee shop employee	• A table • Chairs

The Script

Charlie: Hi, Brenda. Meet my friend Rita.

Brenda: Excuse me, what's your name?

Rita: It's Rita, spelled R-i-t-a.

Brenda: Nice to meet you, Rita.

Charlie: Rita and I work together.

Ned: Hi, Brenda. Can I get you some coffee?

Rita: Brenda, who is this handsome guy?

KEEP GOING!

Watch your classmates' role-plays. Write the answers to these questions:
Who is the handsome guy? What do Charlie, Brenda, and Rita want to drink?

Reasons to Learn English

1. Read the question. Mark your answers with a check (✓).
2. Interview 3–9 classmates. Check your classmates' answers.

Why do you want to learn English?	My Answers	My Classmates' Answers								
		1	2	3	4	5	6	7	8	9
talk to a doctor										
listen to music										
ask for directions										
talk with friends and coworkers										
read stories to my children										

3. Use the chart above to complete the bar graph.

Number of Classmates					
10					
9					
8					
7					
6					
5					
4					
3					
2					
1					
	talk to a doctor	listen to music	ask for directions	talk with friends and coworkers	read stories to my children

KEEP GOING!

Discuss this information with your class. Write 5 sentences.
6 students want to talk with friends and coworkers in English.

Lessons in Learning English

The Project: Create a *Lessons in Learning English* book
Materials: construction paper, markers, a stapler, and scissors

Read stories.

1. Work with 3–5 students. Introduce yourself.

2. Choose your job.

> **Leader:** Help your group work together.
> **Timekeeper:** Watch the time.
> **Recorder:** Write the team's ideas.
> **Reporter:** Tell the class about the project.
> **Supplier:** Get the supplies.

3. Brainstorm the answer to this question: How can you learn English?

> **Timekeeper:** Give the team 5 minutes.
> **Leader:** Ask each person the question.
> **Recorder:** Write the name and answers for each team member.

4. Make the book.

> **Supplier:** Get the supplies from your teacher.
> **Team:** Make 5 pages for your book. Draw and write 1 way to learn English on each page.
> **Recorder:** Make a cover for your book. The book's name is *Lessons in Learning English*.

5. Show your project to the class.

> **Reporter:** Tell the class about the book.
> *These are ways to learn English: go on the Internet, practice with a friend, look up words in a dictionary, listen to the teacher, and watch English movies.*

KEEP GOING!
What are the 5 best ideas from your class?

Picture Cards

1. Cut apart the picture cards. Use the word list to write the words on the back.

2. Work with a partner.

Partner A: Show the picture card to your partner.

Partner B: Say the words.

3. Change roles.

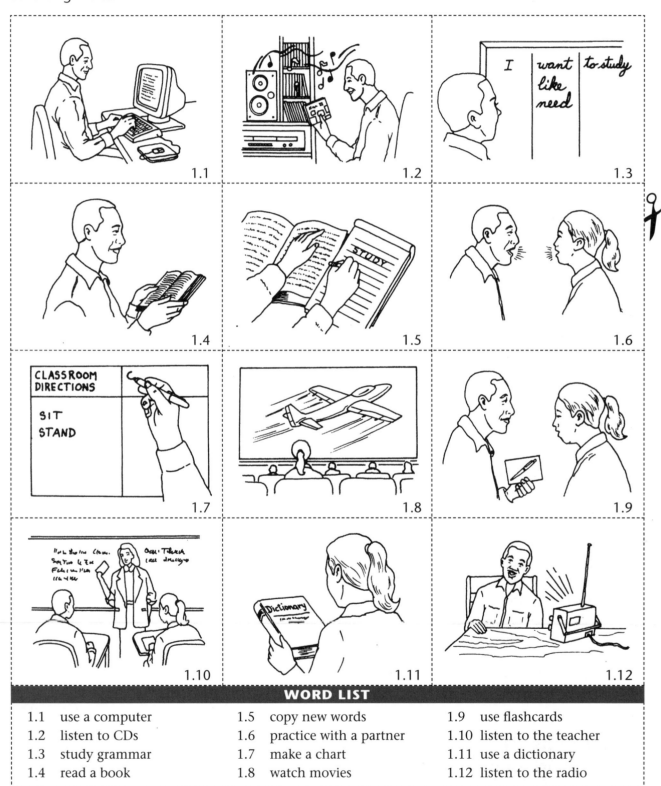

		1.1
		1.2
		1.3
		1.4
		1.5
		1.6
CLASSROOM DIRECTIONS / SIT STAND / 1.7		1.8
		1.9
	Dictionary / 1.11	1.10
		1.12

WORD LIST

1.1 use a computer	1.5 copy new words	1.9 use flashcards
1.2 listen to CDs	1.6 practice with a partner	1.10 listen to the teacher
1.3 study grammar	1.7 make a chart	1.11 use a dictionary
1.4 read a book	1.8 watch movies	1.12 listen to the radio

Grid Game

1. Cut apart the picture cards from page 24.

2. Work with a partner. Don't show your paper to your partner.

Partner A: Put a picture on a square on the grid. Use the picture and the phrase in the square to make a sentence. Tell your partner the sentence: *Sam needs to read a book.*

Partner B: Listen to your partner. Put the picture on the correct square. Check what you hear: *Sam needs to what?*

3. When your grids are full, look at them. Are they the same?

Yes: change roles. No: try again.

Sam needs to	Sam wants to	Sam likes to
Naomi doesn't need to	Naomi doesn't want to	Naomi doesn't like to
Dana and Ahmed need to	Dana and Ahmed want to	Dana and Ahmed like to
Brenda and Linda don't need to	Brenda and Linda don't want to	Brenda and Linda don't like to

Sentence Maker

1. Work with a group of 3 or 4 students. Cut apart the cards.

2. Choose a Recorder.

3. Use the word cards to make 10 different sentences or questions in 10 minutes.
The Recorder writes the group's sentences and questions.

SHE	YOU	WE	NEED
NEEDS	LIKE	LIKES	DON'T
DOESN'T	GRAMMAR	STUDY	DO
DOES	ALONE	WHAT	WHERE
WHEN	TO	.	?

Unit 2 Getting Together

How Do You Feel When It Rains?

1. Work with 3 classmates.

2. Label what you see in the picture.

3. Check your spelling in a dictionary.

KEEP GOING!

Talk about how you feel in different kinds of weather. When do you feel sleepy? Cheerful? Upset?

Enjoy the Weather

1. Work with a partner. Look at the pictures. Match the sentences to the pictures.

2. Partner A: Say the sentences.

   Partner B: Act out the sentences. Use actions and words.

3. Change roles.

_1_ It's sunny. You're cheerful.

_____ Watch the snowstorm outside. You're bored.

_____ Here's 1 million dollars. You're surprised.

_____ The temperature is 32°F. You're cold.

_____ You can't see anything. You're frustrated.

_____ Get out of bed. It's raining. You're sleepy.

_____ The tree fell on your car! You're upset.

_____ The temperature is 98°F. You're hot.

KEEP GOING!

Work in a group. Take turns. Act out the sentences. Say what your classmate is doing.

Tara's Busy Year

Partner A
• **Read a sentence to Partner B.** • **Answer Partner B's question.** • **Watch Partner B write.**
1. Tara will have a busy year. 2. She won't be bored. 3. She will visit friends in June. 4. She will take an English class in August.
• **Listen to Partner B.** • **Check what you hear. Ask:** *She'll what?* **or** *She won't what?* • **Write the sentence.**
5.
6.
7.
8.

- FOLD HERE -

Partner B
• **Listen to Partner A.** • **Check what you hear. Ask:** *She'll what?* **or** *She won't what?* • **Write the sentence.**
1.
2.
3.
4.
• **Read a sentence to Partner A.** • **Answer Partner A's question.** • **Watch Partner A write.**
5. Tara will start school in September. 6. She won't be frustrated. 7. She will take computer classes in November. 8. She will need a vacation in December.

KEEP GOING!

Write 4 sentences about other things Tara will do. How will she feel?
Talk about your sentences with your class.
She will work every day. She will be busy.

Is That Right . . . or Left?

1. Work with 3 classmates. Say all the lines in the script.

2. Choose your character.

3. Finish the conversation. Write more lines for each character.

4. Practice the lines.

5. Act out the role-play with your group.

Scene

On a city street,
2 people are giving 2 tourists
directions.

Characters

- Person 1
- Person 2
- Tourist 1
- Tourist 2

Props

A city map

The Script

Person 1: Are you lost?

Tourist 1: Yes, how can we get to the music festival?

Person 1: It's at Bridge Street Park.

Person 2: Take the train, get off at Second Street, go under the bridge, and turn left.

Person 1: No, turn right and go over the bridge.

Tourist 2: I see. Go to Second Street and turn right.

Tourist 1: Then we go over the bridge.

Person 2: Right!

Tourist 2: Now, where's a good restaurant? We're hungry!

KEEP GOING!

Watch your classmates' role-plays. Write the answers to these questions: How can the tourists get to a good restaurant? Does Person 2 give good directions?

Let's Talk Small Talk

1. Read the question. Mark your answers with a check (✓).
2. Interview 3–9 classmates. Check your classmates' answers.

What are your favorite small-talk topics?	My Answers	My Classmates' Answers								
		1	2	3	4	5	6	7	8	9
sports										
weather										
movies										
music										
television										
family										
school										

3. Use the chart above to complete the bar graph.

Number of Classmates							
10							
9							
8							
7							
6							
5							
4							
3							
2							
1							
	sports	weather	movies	music	television	family	school

KEEP GOING!
Discuss this information with your class. Write 5 sentences.
3 students like to talk about music.

Important Holidays and Events

The Project: Create a monthly holiday and activity calendar
Materials: poster board, markers, stickers, crayons, and colored pencils

February

S	M	T	W	TH	F	S
			1	2	3	4
5	6	7	8	9	10	11
12	13	14 Valentine's Day	15	16	17	18
19	20 President's Day No Class!	21	22	23	24	25
26	27	28 Ana's Birthday Party	29			

1. Work with 3–5 students. Introduce yourself.

2. Choose your job.

   Supplier: Get the supplies.
   Leader: Help your group work together.
   Timekeeper: Watch the time.
   Recorder: Write the team's ideas.
   Reporter: Tell the class about the project.

3. Choose a month. Brainstorm answers to this question: What holidays and activities are important that month?

   Timekeeper: Give the team 5 minutes.
   Leader: Ask each person the question.
   Recorder: Write the name and answers for each team member.

4. Make the calendar.

   Supplier: Get the supplies from your teacher.
   Team: Make a holiday and activity calendar. Write important activities
   and holidays on the correct date. Draw a picture for each holiday.
   Recorder: Put the name of your month at the top of the poster.

5. Show your project to the class.

   Reporter: Tell the class about the poster.
   These are important holidays and activities for next month. Valentine's Day will be on Tuesday,
   February 14th. President's Day will be on Monday, February 20th. Ana's birthday party will be
   on Tuesday, February 20th.

KEEP GOING!
Write 3 sentences about the calendar. What will you and your classmates do?

Picture Cards

1. Cut apart the picture cards. Use the word list to write the words on the back.

2. Work with a partner.

   Partner A: Show the picture card to your partner.

   Partner B: Say the word.

3. Change roles.

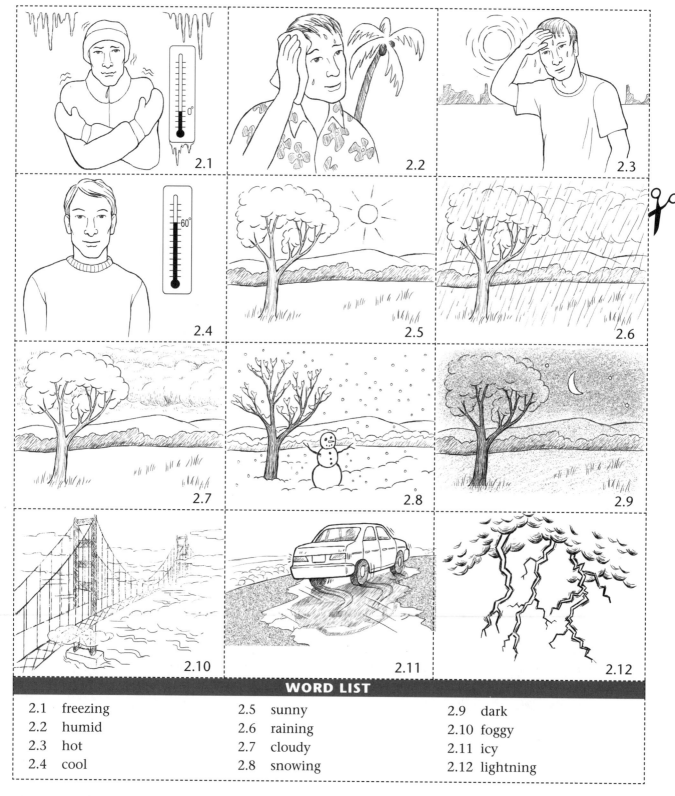

WORD LIST					
2.1	freezing	2.5	sunny	2.9	dark
2.2	humid	2.6	raining	2.10	foggy
2.3	hot	2.7	cloudy	2.11	icy
2.4	cool	2.8	snowing	2.12	lightning

Grid Game

1. Cut apart the picture cards from page 34.

2. Work with a partner. Don't show your paper to your partner.

Partner A: Put a picture on a square on the grid. Use the picture and the phrase in the square to make a sentence. Tell your partner the sentences: *It's sunny. I think I'll go to the park.*

Partner B: Listen to your partner. Put the picture on the correct square. Check what you hear: *You'll what?*

3. When your grids are full, look at them. Are they the same?

Yes: change roles. No: try again.

go to the park	have a picnic	visit a friend
go to the music festival	go to the video store	stay inside the house
go to a baseball game	stay at the library	go see a movie
stay at work	stay home for dinner	go to Florida

Sentence Maker

1. Work with a group of 3 or 4 students. Cut apart the cards.

2. Choose a Recorder.

3. Use the word cards to make 10 different sentences or questions in 10 minutes.
The Recorder writes the group's sentences and questions.

THEY	SHE	WEATHER	WILL
WON'T	WHERE	WHEN	COOL
VISIT	FEBRUARY	AUGUST	CHEERFUL
BORED	HOT	BE	FESTIVAL
THE	IN	.	?

Unit 3 Moving Out

Household Headaches

1. Work with 3 classmates.

2. Label what you see in the picture.

3. Check your spelling in a dictionary.

broken door

KEEP GOING!

Talk about other household problems. Who do you call to fix them?

Looking for Two Bedrooms

1. Work with a partner. Look at the pictures. Match the sentences to the pictures.

2. **Partner A:** Say the sentences.

　　Partner B: Act out the sentences. Use actions and words.

3. Change roles.

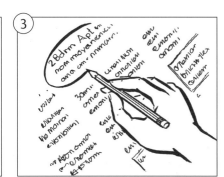
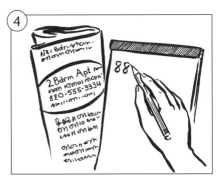

_____ Write down the phone number.　　　　_____ Look for a two-bedroom apartment.

_____ Circle the ad.　　　　　　　　　　　　_____ Count the number of bedrooms.

_____ Look at the neighborhood.　　　　　　_1_ Buy a newspaper. Look at the housing ads.

_____ Ask about the apartment.　　　　　　　_____ Call the number.

KEEP GOING!

Work in a group. Take turns. Act out the sentences. Say what your classmate is doing.

They Like Where They Live

Partner A
• **Read a sentence to Partner B.** • **Answer Partner B's question.** • **Watch Partner B write.**
1. Fernando's apartment is larger than Tony's small house. 2. His apartment is bigger and cheaper. 3. It is quieter and more comfortable. 4. It is his dream apartment.
• **Listen to Partner B.** • **Check what you hear. Ask:** *Can you repeat that?* • **Write the sentence.**
5.
6.
7.
8.

- FOLD HERE -

Partner B
• **Listen to Partner A.** • **Check what you hear. Ask:** *Can you repeat that?* • **Write the sentence.**
1.
2.
3.
4.
• **Read a sentence to Partner A.** • **Answer Partner A's question.** • **Watch Partner A write.**
5. Tony's house is smaller than Fernando's apartment. 6. His house is more expensive. 7. It is sunnier and more convenient. 8. It is his dream house.

KEEP GOING!

Write 4 sentences about other ways to compare a house pend an apartment.
Talk about your sentences with your class.
A smaller house is better than a larger apartment.

One Bedroom or Two?

1. Work with 3 classmates. Say all the lines in the script.

2. Choose your character.

3. Finish the conversation. Write more lines for each character.

4. Practice the lines.

5. Act out the role-play with your group.

Scene	Characters	Props
Inside an apartment building	• Real Estate Agent • Landlord • Terry • Chris, Terry's classmate	Apartment ads from the newspaper classified section

The Script

Real Estate Agent: My client is looking for an apartment.

Landlord: I have 1 apartment for rent.

Terry: I need 2 bedrooms.

Landlord: The apartment has 2 bedrooms and 1 bathroom.

Terry: But the ad says 2 bedrooms and 2 bathrooms.

Landlord: That's a mistake. It's 2 bedrooms and 1 bathroom.

Chris: Hi, Terry. I live in this apartment building.

Real Estate Agent: It looks like a good place to live.

Chris: It is, and the rent is cheap.

KEEP GOING!

Watch your classmates' role-plays. Write the answers to these questions:
How much is the rent? Why does Chris like the apartment?

Where Do You Want to Live?

1. Read the question. Mark your answers with a check (✓).
2. Interview 3–9 classmates. Check your classmates' answers.

Where do you want to live?	My Answers	My Classmates' Answers								
		1	2	3	4	5	6	7	8	9
in the city										
in the country										
in the South										
in the Midwest										
on the East Coast										
on the West Coast										

3. Use the chart above to complete the bar graph.

Number of Classmates						
10						
9						
8						
7						
6						
5						
4						
3						
2						
1						
	in the city	in the country	in the South	in the Midwest	on the East Coast	on the West Coast

KEEP GOING!

Discuss this information with your class. Write 5 sentences.

5 students want to live in the country.

The Perfect Home

The Project: Create a newspaper ad for the perfect home
Materials: construction paper, notebook paper, crayons, markers,
or use a word processing program, if computers are available

For Rent
The Perfect Home
5 BR house, 2 BA
large kit, LR,
DR, and fireplace
$950/mo.

1. Work with 3–5 students. Introduce yourself.

2. Choose your job.

> **Leader:** Help your group work together.
> **Timekeeper:** Watch the time.
> **Recorder:** Write the team's ideas.
> **Reporter:** Tell the class about the project.
> **Supplier:** Get the supplies.

3. Brainstorm the answer to this question: What is the perfect home?

> **Timekeeper:** Give the team 5 minutes.
> **Leader:** Ask each person the question.
> **Recorder:** Write the name and answers for each team member.

4. Make the newspaper ad.

> **Supplier:** Get the supplies from your teacher.
> **Team:** Make a newspaper ad to describe the perfect home. Give the rent, number
> of bedrooms, number of bathrooms, if it's a house or an apartment, and other words
> that describe the perfect home.
> **Recorder:** Write the title for the newspaper ad.

5. Show your project to the class.

> **Reporter:** Tell the class about the newspaper ad.
> *The perfect home has 5 bedrooms, 2 bathrooms, big rooms, and a beautiful kitchen.*

KEEP GOING!
Look at another group's ad. Write what the abbreviations in the ad mean.

Picture Cards

1. Cut apart the picture cards. Use the word list to write the words on the back.

2. Work with a partner.

   Partner A: Show the picture card to your partner.

   Partner B: Say the word.

3. Change roles.

	WORD LIST	
3.1 small	3.5 crowded	3.9 safe
3.2 big	3.6 comfortable	3.10 dangerous
3.3 sunny	3.7 expensive	3.11 quiet
3.4 dark	3.8 cheap	3.12 noisy

Grid Game

1. Cut apart the picture cards from page 44.

2. Work with a partner. Don't show your paper to your partner.

Partner A: Put a picture on a square on the grid. Use the picture and the phrase in the square to make a sentence. Tell your partner the sentence: *The apartment in New York is noisy.*

Partner B: Listen to your partner. Put the picture on the correct square. Check what you hear: *Did you say noisy or sunny?*

3. When your grids are full, look at them. Are they the same?

Yes: change roles. No: try again.

the apartment in Houston	the apartment in San Francisco	Chris' apartment
Teresa's apartment	Tony's apartment	Fernando's apartment
the new apartment	the old apartment	the apartment in Chicago
the apartment in Tampa	the apartment in Flagstaff	the apartment in New York

Sentence Maker

1. Work with a group of 3 or 4 students. Cut apart the cards.

2. Choose a Recorder.

3. Use the word cards to make 10 different sentences or questions in 10 minutes.
The Recorder writes the group's sentences and questions.

SHE	REPAIR PERSON	HE	IS
FIXING	REPAIRING	LEAKING PIPES	BATHROOM
KITCHEN	CRACKED WINDOW	QUIETER	SMALLER
BIGGER	WALL	LOCK	DOOR
THE	THAN	.	?

Unit 4 Looking for Work

What's Your Job?

1. Work with 3 classmates.

2. Label the jobs you see in the picture.

3. Check your spelling in a dictionary.

KEEP GOING!

Talk about other jobs. What jobs are interesting to you?

I Have an Interview!

1. Work with a partner. Look at the pictures. Match the sentences to the pictures.

2. **Partner A:** Say the sentences.

   Partner B: Act out the sentences. Use actions and words.

3. Change roles.

_____ Write questions.

_____ Shake hands.

_1_ Look for information about the company.

_____ Complete the job application.

_____ Wear nice clothes. Look in the mirror.

_____ Check the time. Don't be late for the interview.

_____ Answer all the questions.

_____ Smile and be cheerful.

KEEP GOING!
Work in a group. Take turns. Act out the sentences. Say what your classmate is doing.

Adam and Ana Didn't Get the Jobs

Partner A
• **Read a sentence to Partner B.** • **Answer Partner B's question.** • **Watch Partner B write.**
1. Adam and Ana went on job interviews yesterday. 2. Ana had 5 of years experience. 3. Adam wrote computer programs. 4. They took classes in English.
• **Listen to Partner B.** • **Check what you hear. Ask: *What happened?*** • **Write the sentence.**
5.
6.
7.
8.

- FOLD HERE -

Partner B
• **Listen to Partner A.** • **Check what you hear. Ask: *What happened?*** • **Write the sentence.**
1.
2.
3.
4.
• **Read a sentence to Partner A.** • **Answer Partner A's question.** • **Watch Partner A write.**
5. Adam and Ana arrived late for the interview. 6. Ana didn't look at the interviewer. 7. Adam felt nervous. 8. They didn't get the jobs.

KEEP GOING!

Write 4 sentences about what Adam and Ana did after their interviews.
Talk about your sentences with your class.
Ana ate dinner with her friend at Fran's Restaurant.

Education, Experience, and References

1. Work with 2 classmates. Say all the lines in the script.

2. Choose your character.

3. Finish the conversation. Write more lines for each character.

4. Practice the lines.

5. Act out the role-play with your group.

Scene	Characters 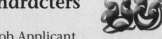	Props 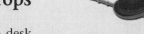
A busy office	• Job Applicant • Job Interviewer 1 • Job Interviewer 2	• A desk • Three chairs • A clipboard • A pen

The Script

Job Applicant: I'm looking for a job.

Job Interviewer 1: We can help you find a job.

Job Interviewer 2: Did you graduate from college?

Job Applicant: Yes, I graduated from college, and I have computer training.

Job Interviewer 1: How much experience do you have?

Job Applicant: I worked with a computer software company for 3 years.

Job Interviewer 2: Do you have any special skills?

Job Interviewer 1: When are you available to work?

KEEP GOING!

Watch your classmates' role-plays. Write the answers to these questions: What are the job applicant's special skills? When is the job applicant available to work?

Good Skills Are Important

1. Read the question. Mark your answers with a check (✓).
2. Interview 3–9 classmates. Check your classmates' answers.

What is most important in a job applicant?	My Answers	My Classmates' Answers								
		1	2	3	4	5	6	7	8	9
education and training										
job experience										
good references										
computer skills										
nice clothes										

3. Use the chart above to complete the bar graph.

Number of Classmates					
10					
9					
8					
7					
6					
5					
4					
3					
2					
1					
	education and training	job experience	good references	computer skills	nice clothes

KEEP GOING!

Discuss this information with your class. Write 5 sentences.
3 students think good references are the most important.

Job Qualifications

The Project: Create a graphic organizer about a job
Materials: poster board, crayons, markers, stickers

1. Work with 3–5 students. Introduce yourself.

2. Choose your job.

> **Leader:** Help your group work together.
> **Timekeeper:** Watch the time.
> **Recorder:** Write the team's ideas.
> **Reporter:** Tell the class about the project.
> **Supplier:** Get the supplies.

3. Talk about your jobs. Decide which team member's job to use.

> **Timekeeper:** Give each team member 1 minute.
> **Leader:** Help everyone talk.

4. Brainstorm the answer to this question: What education, experience, and special skills does my classmate need for his or her job?

> **Timekeeper:** Give the team 5 minutes.
> **Team:** Ask questions to learn what education, experience, and special skills your team member needs for his or her job.
> **Recorder:** Write the answers.

5. Make the graphic organizer.

> **Supplier:** Get the supplies from your teacher.
> **Team:** Make a graphic organizer about the job. Draw a picture of the job in the middle circle and label it. Draw circles around the middle and write in the education, experience, and special skills needed for this job.

6. Show your project to the class.

> **Reporter:** Tell the class about the graphic organizer.
> *A teacher needs a 4-year degree, good communication skills, and experience working with students.*

> **KEEP GOING!**
> Put the graphic organizers on the wall in your classroom or school.
> Be sure to ask permission first.

Picture Cards

1. Cut apart the picture cards. Use the word list to write the words on the back.

2. Work with a partner.

   Partner A: Show the picture card to your partner.

   Partner B: Say the words.

3. Change roles.

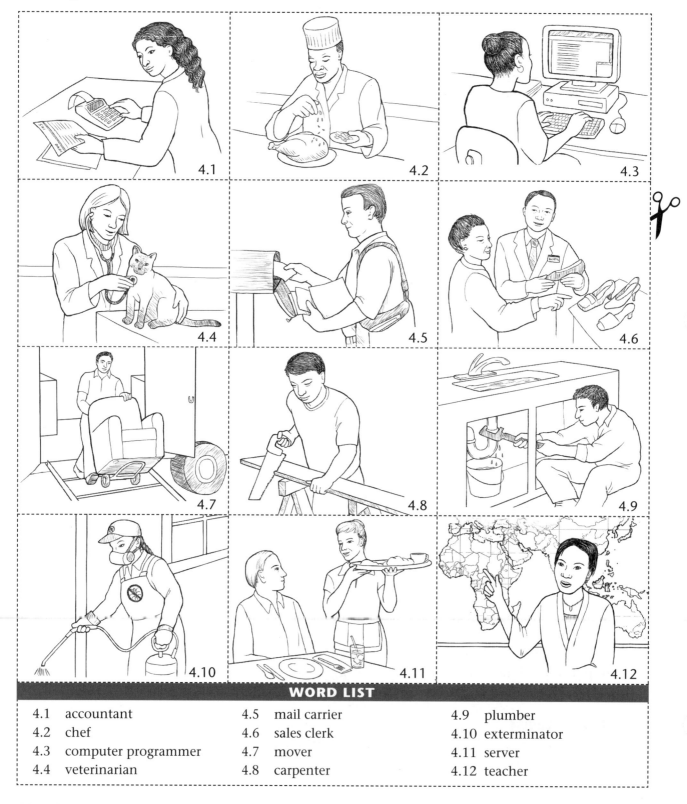

WORD LIST		
4.1 accountant	4.5 mail carrier	4.9 plumber
4.2 chef	4.6 sales clerk	4.10 exterminator
4.3 computer programmer	4.7 mover	4.11 server
4.4 veterinarian	4.8 carpenter	4.12 teacher

Grid Game

1. Cut apart the picture cards from page 54.

2. Work with a partner. Don't show your paper to your partner.

Partner A: Put a picture on a square on the grid. Use the picture and the year in the square to make a sentence. Tell your partner the sentence: *He was a mover in 1995.*

Partner B: Listen to your partner. Put the picture on the correct square. Check what you hear: *When?*

3. When your grids are full, look at them. Are they the same?

Yes: change roles. No: try again.

1995	1996	1997
1998	1999	2000
2001	2002	2003
2004	2005	2006

Sentence Maker

1. Work with a group of 3 or 4 students. Cut apart the cards.

2. Choose a Recorder.

3. Use the word cards to make 10 different sentences or questions in 10 minutes.
The Recorder writes the group's sentences and questions.

THEY	SHE	YOU	FEEL
FELT	WORK	WORKED	TAKE
TOOK	DID	DIDN'T	NERVOUS
CONFIDENT	ENGLISH CLASSES	A STORE	COMPUTER CLASSES
A	AT	.	?

Unit 5 On the Job

This Is Where I Work

1. Work with 3 classmates.

2. Label what you see in the picture.

3. Check your spelling in a dictionary.

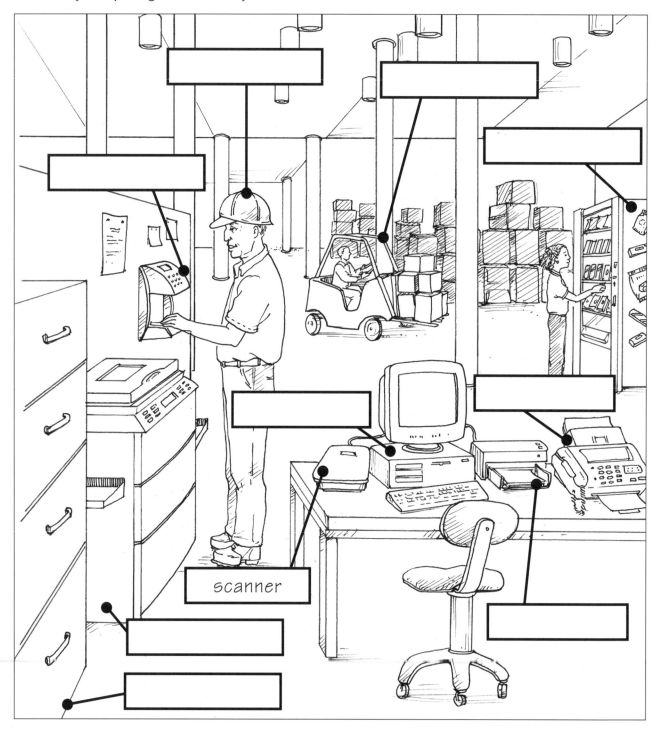

scanner

KEEP GOING!

Talk about the workplace. Where are the workplace machines in this picture?

The computer is on the desk, next to the printer.

On the Job

1. Work with a partner. Look at the pictures. Match the sentences to the pictures.

2. **Partner A:** Say the sentences.

　　Partner B: Act out the sentences. Use actions and words.

3. Change roles.

_____ Smile and wave goodbye.　　　　_____ Put on plastic gloves.

_1_ Put on a hairnet.　　　　　　　　　_____ Make a sandwich.

_____ Give the customer a sandwich.　　_____ Take the money.

_____ Wash your hands.　　　　　　　　_____ Give change back.

KEEP GOING!

Work in a group. Take turns. Act out the sentences. Say what your classmate is doing.

Pablo and Jim Might Get Raises!

Partner A
• **Read a sentence to Partner B.** • **Answer Partner B's question.** • **Watch Partner B write.**
1. Pablo and Jim might get raises this year. 2. Pablo worked very hard this year. 3. Jim was on time for work. 4. They didn't make any mistakes.
• **Listen to Partner B.** • **Check what you hear. Ask: *Can you repeat that, please?*** • **Write the sentence.**
5.
6.
7.
8.

- FOLD HERE -

Partner B
• **Listen to Partner A.** • **Check what you hear. Ask: *Can you repeat that, please?*** • **Write the sentence.**
1.
2.
3.
4.
• **Read a sentence to Partner A.** • **Answer Partner A's question.** • **Watch Partner A write.**
5. Pablo and Jim might not get raises. 6. Pablo was late for work everyday. 7. Jim didn't wear appropriate clothing 8. They didn't make their boss happy.

KEEP GOING!

Write 4 sentences about what you should do to get a raise.
Talk about your sentences with your class.
I should be on time.

I'm Really Busy!

1. Work with 2 classmates. Say all the lines in the script.

2. Choose your character.

3. Finish the conversation. Write more lines for each character.

4. Practice the lines.

5. Act out the role-play with your group.

Scene	Characters	Props
• The boss in his car calling his office on a cell phone • An office	• Boss, Mr. Jones • Office Manager • Administrative Assistant	• A desk with many papers on it • A chair • A cell phone

The Script

Boss: Hello. It's Mr. Jones. I might be late today.

Office Manager: No problem. Please email the company that Mr. Jones might be late.

Administrative Assistant: Did you say Mr. Bones?

Office Manager: No, Mr. Jones.

Administrative Assistant: OK. I'll do it right away.

Boss: Can you please fax the letter on my desk to my accountant? Oh, and I need 3 copies of that letter.

Office Manager: OK, let me repeat all that.

KEEP GOING!

Watch your classmates' role-plays. Write the answers to these questions: How many times does the boss have to repeat the instructions? What other questions does the Office Manager ask?

Be Positive

1. Read the question. Mark your answers with a check (✓).

2. Interview 3–9 classmates. Check your classmates' answers.

Which statements are true for you?	My Answers	My Classmates' Answers								
		1	2	3	4	5	6	7	8	9
I want to learn.										
I want to improve.										
I help others.										
I have a positive attitude.										
I work well with others.										
I look for solutions.										

3. Use the chart above to complete the bar graph.

Number of Classmates	want to learn	want to improve	help others	have a positive attitude	work well with others	look for solutions
10						
9						
8						
7						
6						
5						
4						
3						
2						
1						

KEEP GOING!

Discuss this information with your class. Write 5 sentences about your classmates.
6 students look for solutions.

Work Behavior

The Project: Create a chart about good and bad work behaviors

Materials: poster board or paper, markers, and pens

Good and Bad Work Behavior	
🙂	🙁
1. *smile at customers* 2. *be on time for work* 3. 4. 5. 6.	1. *be negative* 2. *complain* 3. 4. 5. 6.

1. Work with 3–5 students. Introduce yourself.

2. Choose your job.

> **Leader:** Help your group work together.
> **Timekeeper:** Watch the time.
> **Recorder:** Write the team's ideas.
> **Reporter:** Tell the class about the project.
> **Supplier:** Get the supplies.

3. Brainstorm answers to this question: What are examples of good and bad work behavior?

> **Timekeeper:** Give the team 5 minutes.
> **Leader:** Ask each person the question.
> **Recorder:** Write the name and answers for each team member.

4. Make the chart.

> **Supplier:** Get the supplies from your teacher.
> **Team:** Draw two columns, one for good work behaviors and one for bad work behaviors. Write or draw the headings for each column. Write or draw the work behavior in each column.
> **Leader:** Help the team think of a title for the chart.
> **Recorder:** Write the title on the chart.

5. Show your project to your class.

> **Reporter:** Tell the class about the chart.
> *These are good work behaviors: smile at customers and be on time for work.*
> *These are bad work behaviors: be negative and complain.*

KEEP GOING!

Work in your group. Write two paragraphs. In the first paragraph, describe good work behavior. In the second paragraph, describe bad work behavior. Use information from other groups.

Picture Cards

1. Cut apart the picture cards. Use the word list to write the words on the back.

2. Work with a partner.

Partner A: Show the picture card to your partner.

Partner B: Say the words.

3. Change roles.

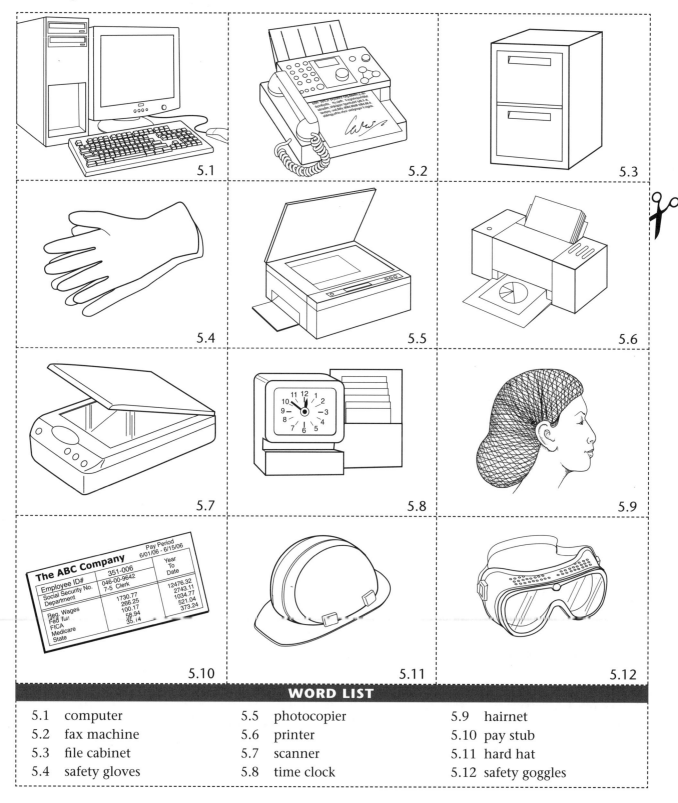

5.1	5.2	5.3
5.4	5.5	5.6
5.7	5.8	5.9
5.10	5.11	5.12

WORD LIST

5.1 computer	5.5 photocopier	5.9 hairnet
5.2 fax machine	5.6 printer	5.10 pay stub
5.3 file cabinet	5.7 scanner	5.11 hard hat
5.4 safety gloves	5.8 time clock	5.12 safety goggles

Grid Game

1. Cut apart the picture cards from page 64.

2. Work with a partner. Don't show your paper to your partner.

Partner A: Put a picture on a square on the grid. Use the picture and the phrase in the square to make a sentence. Tell your partner the sentence: *The computer is next to the window.*

Partner B: Listen to your partner. Put the picture on the correct square. Check what you hear: *Where?*

3. When your grids are full, look at them. Are they the same?

Yes: change roles. No: try again.

in the corner	near the vending machine	at the front of the office
in the back of the office	in the closet	on the floor
to the left of the door	next to the window	in front of the window
on the chair	behind the door	to the right of the door

Sentence Maker

1. Work with a group of 3 or 4 students. Cut apart the cards.

2. Choose a Recorder.

3. Use the word cards to make 10 different sentences or questions in 10 minutes.
   The Recorder writes the group's sentences and questions.

SHE	YOU	THEY	MIGHT
SHOULD	NOT	DO	DOES
BE	TALK	SMILE	FIRED
RAISE	ANGRY	CUSTOMERS	GET
A	AT	.	?

Unit 6 Pick Up the Phone

I'll Call You

1. Work with 3 classmates.

2. Label what you see in the picture.

3. Check your spelling in a dictionary.

KEEP GOING!

Talk about the different types of phones in the picture. What type(s) of phone(s) do you use?

I Missed the Bus!

1. Work with a partner. Look at the pictures. Match the sentences to the pictures.

2. **Partner A:** Say the sentences.

    Partner B: Act out the sentences. Use actions and words.

3. Change roles.

I'm so sorry.

_1_ Wake up and turn off the alarm.

____ Take out your cell phone.

____ Check the bus schedule.

____ Run for the bus. Oh no! You missed it.

____ Take the next bus.

____ Oh, no! You overslept. Get dressed!

____ Dial your work number.

____ Tell the boss you will be late. Apologize.

KEEP GOING!

Work in a group. Take turns. Act out the sentences. Say what your classmate is doing.

     Unit 6 Vocabulary in Action **69**

Let's Go Jogging

Partner A
• **Read a sentence to Partner B.** • **Answer Partner B's question.** • **Watch Partner B write.**
1. Tom was jogging with Nadine this morning at 8:00 a.m. 2. He wasn't driving to work. 3. He wasn't opening the mail at 10:00 p.m. 4. He was sleeping.
• **Listen to Partner B.** • **Check what you hear. Ask:** *What did you say?* • **Write the sentence.**
5.
6.
7.
8.

- Fold Here -

Partner B
• **Listen to Partner A.** • **Check what you hear. Ask:** *What did you say?* • **Write the sentence.**
1.
2.
3.
4.
• **Read a sentence to Partner A.** • **Answer Partner A's question.** • **Watch Partner A write.**
5. Julie was jogging with Andy this morning at 8:00 a.m. 6. She wasn't doing laundry. 7. She wasn't eating dinner at 6:00 p.m. 8. She was going to school.

KEEP GOING!
Write 4 sentences about what you were doing at different times yesterday.
Talk about your sentences with the class.
I was eating lunch at 1:00 p.m.

Pat Isn't Coming in Today

1. Work with 2 classmates. Say all the lines in the script.

2. Choose your character.

3. Finish the conversation. Write more lines for each character.

4. Practice the lines.

5. Act out the role-play with your group.

Scene	Characters	Props
• A house • A restaurant	• Employee 1 • Employee 2, Pat • Manager	• Two telephones • A table • Two chairs

The Script

Employee 1: Hello, Rita's Restaurant. How can I help you?

Employee 2: Can I speak to the manager? This is Pat.

Employee 1: I'm sorry. He's not in yet. May I take a message?

Employee 2: Yes, I'm calling in sick today.

Employee 1: OK, I'll give the manager the message.

Manager: Good evening. Any messages for me?

KEEP GOING!

Watch your classmates' role-plays. Write the answers to these questions:
Is the manager upset? Are there more messages for the manager?

Helping Hands

1. Read the survey questions. Mark your answer with a check (✓).

2. Interview 3–9 classmates. Check your classmates' answers.

What community services do you use?	My Answers	My Classmates' Answers								
		1	**2**	**3**	**4**	**5**	**6**	**7**	**8**	**9**
job centers										
public library										
senior centers										
volunteer centers										
community schools										
emergency rescue (911)										

3. Use the chart above to complete the bar graph.

Number of Classmates						
10						
9						
8						
7						
6						
5						
4						
3						
2						
1						
	job centers	public library	senior centers	volunteer centers	community schools	emergency rescue (911)

KEEP GOING!

Discuss this information with your class. Write 5 sentences.

7 students use the public library.

Community Services

The Project: Create a local community-service poster
Materials: poster board, phone books, markers, crayons,
community newsletters, bulletins, magazines, or Internet search engines
(if available)—keywords: community services for (name of city)

Our Local Community Service		
Community Service	Why You Go There	Local Address/ Phone Number
Public Library	Storytelling hour, check out books, free Internet	40 Oak St. 744-555-1000

1. Work with 3–5 students. Introduce yourself.

2. Choose your job.

> **Leader:** Help your group work together.
> **Timekeeper:** Watch the time.
> **Recorder:** Write the team's ideas.
> **Reporter:** Tell the class about the project.
> **Supplier:** Get the supplies.

3. Brainstorm answers to this question: What are some local community services?

> **Timekeeper:** Give the team 5 minutes.
> **Leader:** Ask each person the question.
> **Recorder:** Write the names and answers for each team member.

4. Make the poster.

> **Supplier:** Get the supplies from your teacher.
> **Team:** Choose one local community service. Find information about your community service: name, local address, telephone number, and why you use this service. Write the information about the community service on the poster.
> **Leader:** Help the team think of a title.
> **Recorder:** Write the title on the poster.

5. Show your project to the class.

> **Reporter:** Tell the class about the project.
> *Our community has a large public library. It is on the corner of Oak and Main.*

> **KEEP GOING!**
> Look at posters from other groups. Compare information. Write down addresses
> and phone numbers for community services you want to use.

Picture Cards

1. Cut apart the picture cards. Use the word list to write the words on the back.

2. Work with a partner.

Partner A: Show the picture card to your partner.

Partner B: Say the words.

3. Change roles.

WORD LIST		
6.1 driving home	6.5 shopping for food	6.9 doing the laundry
6.2 making dinner	6.6 reading the newspaper	6.10 jogging
6.3 eating dinner	6.7 talking on the telephone	6.11 opening a letter
6.4 watching television	6.8 exercising	6.12 faxing a letter

Grid Game

1. Cut apart the picture cards from page 74.

2. Work with a partner. Don't show your paper to your partner.

Partner A: Put a picture on a square on the grid. Use the picture and the time in the square to make a sentence. Tell your partner the sentence: *She was jogging at 7:00 a.m.*

Partner B: Listen to your partner. Put the picture on the correct square. Check what you hear: *She was doing what? When?*

3. When your grids are full, look at them. Are they the same?

Yes: change roles. No: try again.

7:00 a.m.	9:30 a.m.	10:15 a.m.
noon (12:00 p.m.)	1:00 p.m.	3:00 p.m.
7:00 p.m.	9:13 p.m.	10:50 p.m.
midnight (12:00 a.m.)	1:00 a.m.	6:15 a.m.

Sentence Maker

1. Work with a group of 3 or 4 students. Cut apart the cards.

2. Choose a Recorder.

3. Use the word cards to make 10 different sentences or questions in 10 minutes.
The Recorder writes the group's sentences and questions.

SHE	I	THEY	WAS
WERE	WASN'T	WEREN'T	DRIVING
DOING	SHOPPING	WATCHING	SLEEPING
HOME	WHAT	WHEN	TELEVISION
9:00 A.M.	AT	.	?

Unit 7 What's for Dinner?

Do We Have All the Ingredients?

1. Sit with 3 classmates.

2. Work together. Label what you see in the picture.

3. Check your spelling in a dictionary.

jar of peanut butter

PEANUT BUTTER COOKIES

1 Gal.

1QT. 1QT.

5 LBS.

1 LB.

KEEP GOING!

Talk about food shopping. What do you like to buy?

Smart Savings

1. Work with a partner. Look at the pictures. Match the sentences to the pictures.

2. **Partner A:** Say the sentences.

   Partner B: Act out the sentences. Use actions and words.

3. Change roles.

__1__ You need to buy coffee. Open the newspaper. Look at the ads.

_____ Look for a cheaper can of coffee. Put it in your cart.

_____ Drive to the supermarket.

_____ It's too expensive. Put the can down.

_____ Cut out a coupon for coffee.

_____ Pick up 1 can of coffee. Look at the unit price on the shelf.

_____ Give the checker your coupon.

_____ Pay for the coffee and get your receipt. You saved $0.25.

KEEP GOING!

Work in a group. Take turns. Act out the sentences. Say what your classmate is doing.

How Much Does She Need?

Partner A
• **Read a sentence to Partner B.** • **Answer Partner B's question.** • **Watch Partner B write.**
1. Terry needs to buy some food for her recipe. 2. She needs 1 cup of milk. 3. She doesn't need any cheese. 4. She needs 6 potatoes.
• **Listen to Partner B.** • **Check what you hear. Ask:** *How much?* **or** *How many?* • **Write the sentence.**
5.
6.
7.
8.

- FOLD HERE -

Partner B
• **Listen to Partner A.** • **Check what you hear. Ask:** *How much?* **or** *How many?* • **Write the sentence.**
1.
2.
3.
4.
• **Read a sentence to Partner A.** • **Answer Partner A's question.** • **Watch Partner A write.**
5. Terry doesn't need to buy any vegetables for her salad. 6. She has 2 onions. 7. She has 8 large mushrooms. 8. She has 3 tomatoes.

KEEP GOING!

Write 4 sentences about what other foods Terry needs. Talk about your
sentences with your class.
She needs 3 apples.

It's on the List

1. Work with 3 classmates. Say all the lines in the script.

2. Choose your character.

3. Finish the conversation. Write more lines for each character.

4. Practice the lines.

5. Act out the role-play with your group.

Scene	Characters 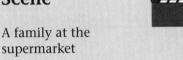	Props
A family at the supermarket	• Dad • Mom • Teenager • Store Clerk	• Shopping list • Food items • Pencil or pen

The Script

Dad: Did you bring the shopping list?

Mom: Yes, I have it.

Dad: We need a loaf of bread.

Teenager: Do you have candy bars on the list?

Mom: Excuse me, where's the bread, please?

Store Clerk: Bread? It's in aisle 5, next to the soup.

Teenager: And where are the candy bars?

Mom: Is candy on the list?

KEEP GOING!

Watch your classmates' role-plays. Write the answers to these questions:
Does the teenager get the candy bars? What else does the family need?

Healthy Habits

1. Read the survey question. Mark your answer with a check (✓).

2. Interview 3–9 classmates. Check your classmates' answers.

Do you eat _____?	My Answers	My Classmates' Answers								
		1	2	3	4	5	6	7	8	9
spinach										
oranges										
low-fat yogurt										
chocolate										
whole-grain bread										
lean meat										

3. Use the chart above to complete the bar graph.

Number of Classmates						
10						
9						
8						
7						
6						
5						
4						
3						
2						
1						
	spinach	oranges	low-fat yogurt	chocolate	whole-grain bread	lean meat

KEEP GOING!

Discuss this information with your class. Write 5 sentences.

4 students eat whole-grain bread. They have a healthy diet.

Eating Right

The Project: Share a healthy recipe
Materials: chart paper, markers, crayons, pens, and pencils, or create recipe cards on the computer

Fresh and Chunky Salsa
Serves 8, 1/4 cup per serving

1 14 1/2-ounce can chopped tomatoes   1 tablespoon vinegar
1/2 cup chopped green or yellow pepper   1/2 teaspoon ground cumin
2 green onions, sliced   1/2 teaspoon garlic
2 tablespoons fresh cilantro or parsley   a few dashes bottled red hot pepper sauce

In a bowl, stir together all ingredients. Serve with low-fat tortilla chips. It can be covered and stored in the refrigerator for up to 1 week.

1. Work with 3–5 students. Introduce yourself.

2. Choose your job.

> **Leader:** Help your group work together.
> **Timekeeper:** Watch the time.
> **Recorder:** Write the team's ideas.
> **Reporter:** Tell the class about the project.
> **Supplier:** Get the supplies.

3. Brainstorm the answers to this question: What is your favorite healthy recipe?

> **Timekeeper:** Give the team 5 minutes.
> **Leader:** Ask each person the question.
> **Recorder:** Write the names and answers for each team member.

4. Make a recipe card.

> **Supplier:** Get the supplies from your teacher.
> **Team:** Choose a healthy recipe. Write the recipe. Draw pictures of ingredients or the final product.
> **Leader:** Help the team think of a title for the recipe.
> **Recorder:** Write the title of the recipe.

5. Show your project to the class.

> **Reporter:** Tell the class about the recipe.
> *Our healthy recipe is for salsa made with tomatoes, onions, garlic, and peppers.*

> **KEEP GOING!**
> Which group's recipe is the healthiest? The least expensive? The most unusual?

Picture Cards

1. Cut apart the picture cards. Use the word list to write the words on the back.

2. Work with a partner.

   Partner A: Show the picture card to your partner.

   Partner B: Say the words.

3. Change roles.

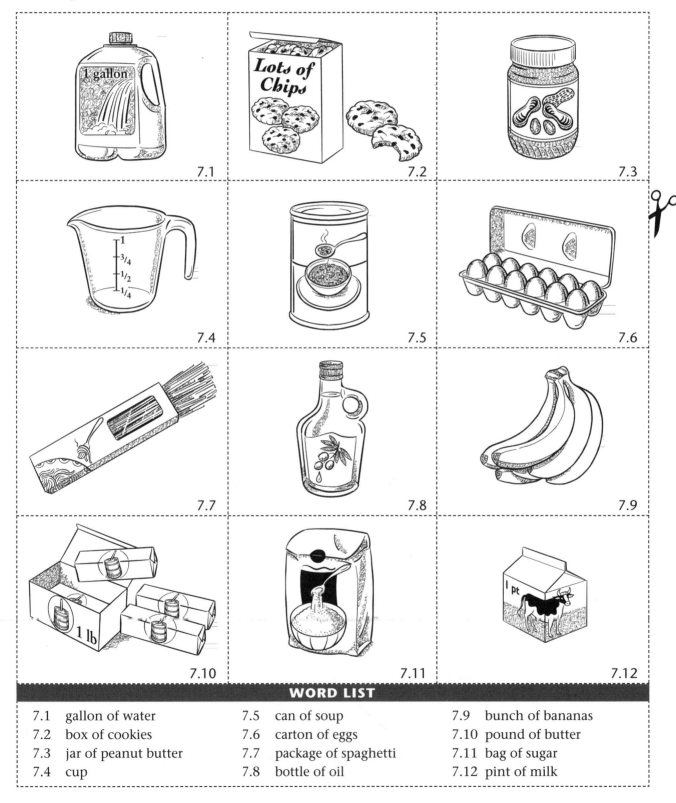

WORD LIST

7.1 gallon of water	7.5 can of soup	7.9 bunch of bananas
7.2 box of cookies	7.6 carton of eggs	7.10 pound of butter
7.3 jar of peanut butter	7.7 package of spaghetti	7.11 bag of sugar
7.4 cup	7.8 bottle of oil	7.12 pint of milk

Grid Game

1. Cut apart the picture cards from page 84.

2. Work with a partner. Don't show your paper to your partner.

Partner A: Put a picture on a square on the grid. Use the picture and the price on the grid to make a sentence. Tell your partner the sentence: *A gallon of water costs $1.49.*

Partner B: Listen to your partner. Put the picture on the correct square. Check what you hear: *How much does it cost?*

3. When your grids are full, look at them. Are they the same? Yes: change roles. No: try again.

$1.49	$1.59	$1.65
$1.89	$1.99	$2.79
$2.85	$3.35	$3.50
$4.49	$5.00	$6.99

Sentence Maker

1. Work with a group of 3 or 4 students. Cut apart the cards.

2. Choose a Recorder.

3. Use the word cards to make 10 different sentences or questions in 10 minutes.
The Recorder writes the group's sentences and questions.

SHE	I	YOU	HOW
MANY	SOME	ANY	DON'T
DOESN'T	NEED	NEEDS	MILK
MUCH	CHEESE	APPLES	HAVE
HAS	DO	.	?

Unit 8 Stay Safe and Well

Get Well Soon

1. Work with 3 classmates.

2. Label what you see in the picture.

3. Check your spelling in a dictionary.

KEEP GOING!

Talk about each person in the picture. What are the symptoms? What are the illnesses?

What's the Problem?

1. Work with a partner. Look at the pictures. Match the sentences to the pictures.

2. **Partner A:** Say the sentences.

  Partner B: Act out the sentences. Use actions and words.

3. Change roles.

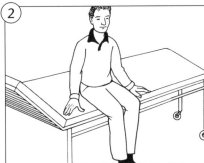

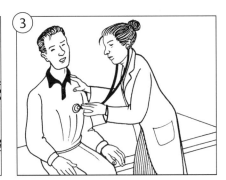

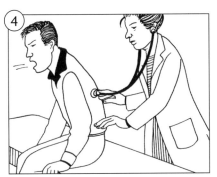

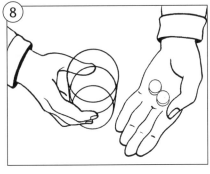

_____ Sit down.

_____ Breathe out.

_____ Open your mouth.

_____ Take a deep breath.

_____ Say, "Ahh."

_____ Lie down.

_1_ Show me where it hurts.

_____ Take two pain relievers.

KEEP GOING!
Work in a group. Take turns. Act out the sentences. Say what your classmate is doing.

Something Happened to Megan and Brian!

Partner A
• **Read a sentence to Partner B.** • **Answer Partner B's question.** • **Watch Partner B write.**
1. Megan was driving when she had an accident. 2. She broke her arm. 3. She cut her leg, too. 4. She didn't hurt her back.
• **Listen to Partner B.** • **Check what you hear. Say:** *Excuse me?* • **Write the sentence.**
5.
6.
7.
8.

- Fold Here -

Partner B
• **Listen to Partner A.** • **Check what you hear. Say:** *Excuse me?* • **Write the sentence.**
1.
2.
3.
4.
• **Read a sentence to Partner A.** • **Answer Partner A's question.** • **Watch Partner A write.**
5. Brian hurt his back. 6. He was playing soccer when it happened. 7. He also fell and cut his arm. 8. He didn't break his leg.

KEEP GOING!

Write 4 sentences about when you were hurt. What were you doing?
Talk about your sentences with the class.
I was playing tennis when I hurt my ankle.

A Headache at the Pharmacy

1. Work with 2 classmates. Say all the lines in the script.

2. Choose your character.

3. Finish the conversation. Write more lines for each character.

4. Practice the lines.

5. Act out the role-play with your group.

Scene	Characters	Props
A pharmacy	• Customer 1 • Pharmacist • Customer 2	• Table or counter • Pill bottle with prescription label • Doctor's prescription

The Script

Customer 1: I'd like to have this prescription filled, please.

Pharmacist: Is the prescription for you?

Customer 1: Yes. It's for pain pills. I get terrible headaches when I'm at work.

Customer 2: I have the same problem. But I was using the computer at home when my headaches started.

Pharmacist: Let me fill this for you right away.

Customer 2: Could you refill this prescription, please?

Pharmacist: Just a moment, please. Here is your prescription. Four pills, once a day.

Customer 1: That can't be right!

KEEP GOING!

Watch your classmates' role-plays. Write the answers to these questions: Did the pharmacist give Customer 1 the right prescription? What questions does the pharmacist ask Customer 2?

Unit 8 Role-Play **91**

First Aid

1. Read the survey questions. Mark your answer with a check (✓).

2. Interview 3–9 classmates. Check your classmates' answers.

What do you do when you are sick?	My Answers	My Classmates' Answers								
		1	2	3	4	5	6	7	8	9
eat chicken soup										
sleep										
take pain relievers										
go to the doctor										
take vitamins										
take prescription medicine										

3. Use the chart above to complete the bar graph.

Number of Classmates						
10						
9						
8						
7						
6						
5						
4						
3						
2						
1						
	eat chicken soup	sleep	take pain relievers	go to the doctor	take vitamins	take prescription medicine

KEEP GOING!

Discuss this information with your class. Write 5 sentences.

3 students take pain relievers.

Illnesses and Symptoms

The Project: Create a concentration game
Materials: index cards, pens, markers, and crayons

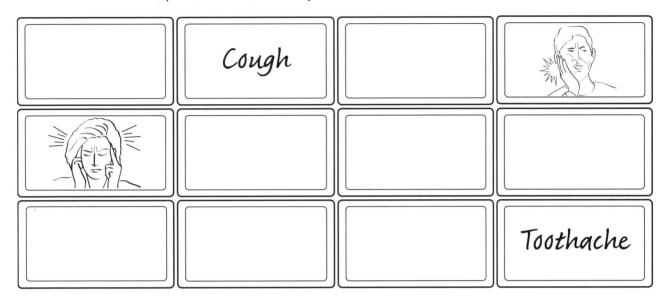

1. Work with 3–5 students. Introduce yourself.

2. Choose your job.

> **Leader:** Help your group work together.
> **Timekeeper:** Watch the time.
> **Recorder:** Write the team's ideas.
> **Reporter:** Tell the class about the project.
> **Supplier:** Get the supplies.

3. Brainstorm answers to this question: What are some illnesses and symptoms?

> **Timekeeper:** Give the team 5 minutes.
> **Leader:** Ask each person the question.
> **Recorder:** Write the name and answers for each team member.

4. Make the concentration game.

> **Supplier:** Get the supplies from your teacher.
> **Team:** Choose 12 illnesses or symptoms for your concentration game.
> • On 1 card write the illness or symptom.
> • On another card draw a matching picture.
> • Make 24 cards total—12 with pictures and 12 with the matching illness or symptom.

5. Show your project to the class.

> **Reporter:** Tell the class about the illnesses and symptoms in your concentration game.
> *The most unusual illness is "English Headache Sickness." The symptoms are a headache*
> *and tired eyes from too much studying.*

> ### KEEP GOING!
> Give your cards to a different group to play the concentration matching game.

Picture Cards

1. Cut apart the picture cards. Use the word list to write the words on the back.

2. Work with a partner.

   Partner A: Show the picture card to your partner.

   Partner B: Say the words.

3. Change roles.

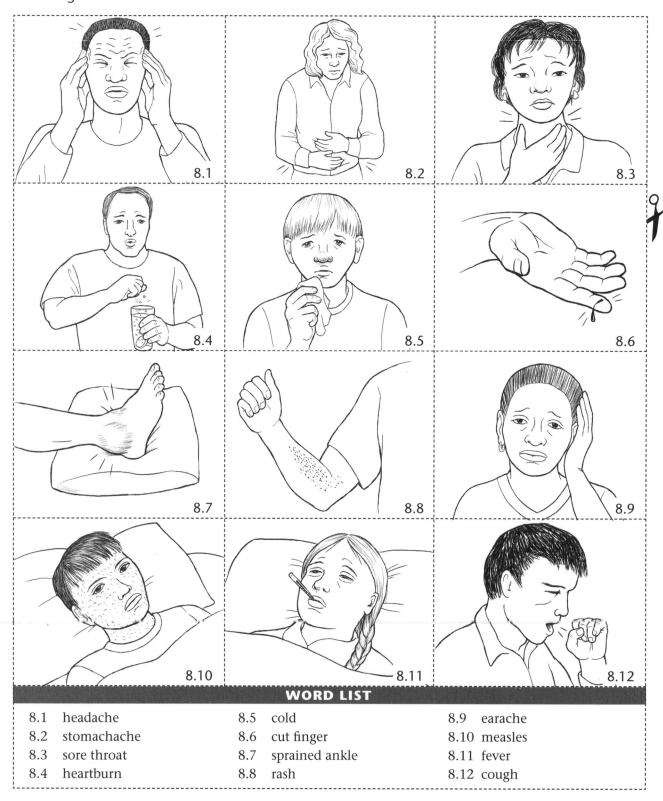

8.1	8.2	8.3
8.4	8.5	8.6
8.7	8.8	8.9
8.10	8.11	8.12

WORD LIST

8.1 headache	8.5 cold	8.9 earache
8.2 stomachache	8.6 cut finger	8.10 measles
8.3 sore throat	8.7 sprained ankle	8.11 fever
8.4 heartburn	8.8 rash	8.12 cough

Grid Game

1. Cut apart the picture cards from page 94.
2. Work with a partner. Don't show your paper to your partner.
   Partner A: Put a picture on a square on the grid. Use the picture and the name in the square to make sentences. Tell your partner the sentences: *Jack has a cough. He needs to see Dr. Smith.*
   Partner B: Listen to your partner. Put the picture on the correct square. Check what you hear: *Why does Jack need to see a doctor?*
3. When your grids are full, look at them. Are they the same?
   Yes: change roles. No: try again.

Dr. Smith	Dr. Sams	Dr. Taylor
Dr. Tyler	Dr. Ross	Dr. Rose
Dr. Jones	Dr. James	Dr. Goode
Dr. Great	Dr. Franks	Dr. Friend

Sentence Maker

1. Work with a group of 3 or 4 students. Cut apart the cards.
2. Choose a Recorder.
3. Use the word cards to make 10 different sentences or questions in 10 minutes.
   The Recorder writes the group's sentences and questions.

BRIAN	HE	HIS	WAS
DOES	WHEN	DRIVING	WORKING
HOW	FELL	HAD	OFTEN
MEDICINE	MUCH	ACCIDENT	TAKE
TO	AN	.	?

Unit 9 Money Matters

At the Bank

1. Work with 3 classmates.

2. Label what you see in the picture.

3. Check your spelling in a dictionary.

KEEP GOING!
Talk about banking services. What banking services do you use?

Painting on a Budget

1. Work with a partner. Look at the pictures. Match the sentences to the pictures.

2. **Partner A:** Say the sentences.

   Partner B: Act out the sentences. Use actions and words.

3. Change roles.

_____ Look at your work. Say, "Great job!"

_____ Paint the ceiling.

_____ Cover the furniture and floor.

_____ Paint the walls.

_____ Climb the ladder. Careful!

__1__ It's time to paint. Open the paint can.

_____ Close up the ladder.

_____ Dip the brush in the paint.

She Bought It and He Returned It

Partner A
• **Read a sentence to Partner B.** • **Answer Partner B's question.** • **Watch Partner B write.**
1. Gina went to the bank to get money. 2. She got money to buy a microwave for Tam. 3. She bought the microwave because Tam needed a new one. 4. Tam's microwave broke because it was old.
• **Listen to Partner B.** • **Check what you hear. Ask:** *Why?* • **Write the sentence.**
5.
6.
7.
8.

- FOLD HERE -

Partner B
• **Listen to Partner A.** • **Check what you hear. Ask:** *Why?* • **Write the sentence.**
1.
2.
3.
4.
• **Read a sentence to Partner A.** • **Answer Partner A's question.** • **Watch Partner A write.**
5. Tam returned the microwave because it was too big. 6. He went back to the store to buy a smaller one. 7. He got money back because it was on sale. 8. He bought Gina a gift with the money.

KEEP GOING!

Write 4 sentences about the gifts Tam bought Gina. Talk about your
sentences with your class.
He bought her a rug because she needed a new one.

Refund or Exchange?

1. Work with 2 classmates. Say all the lines in the script.

2. Choose your character.

3. Finish the conversation. Write more lines for each character.

4. Practice the lines.

5. Act out the role-play with your group.

Scene	Characters	Props
A department store	• Store clerk • Customer 1 • Customer 2	• A shopping receipt • A sweater • A pair of shoes • Play money

The Script

Store Clerk: Can I help you?

Customer 1: I'd like to return this sweater.

Store Clerk: Why are you returning it?

Customer 1: It doesn't fit.

Customer 2: Excuse me. I'd like to exchange these shoes.

Store Clerk: I'll be with you in a moment.

Customer 2: I'm late for school. I need my money back.

Customer 1: I don't have time to wait.

KEEP GOING!

Watch your classmates' role-plays. Write the answers to these questions: Who does the clerk help first? Why does Customer 2 want to exchange the shoes?

You Can't Be Too Careful

1. Read the question. Mark your answers with a check (✓).

2. Interview 3–9 classmates. Check your classmates' answers.

How do you protect your credit cards or ATM card?	My Answers	My Classmates' Answers								
		1	2	3	4	5	6	7	8	9
make a list of card information										
keep my PIN in a safe place										
compare my receipts and bills										
cut up old cards										
never lend my cards to anyone										
do not have credit cards or ATM cards										

3. Use the chart above to complete the bar graph.

Number of Classmates	make a list of card information	keep my PIN in a safe place	compare my receipts and bills	cut up old cards	never lend my cards to anyone	do not have credit cards or ATM cards
10						
9						
8						
7						
6						
5						
4						
3						
2						
1						

KEEP GOING!

Discuss this information with your class. Write 5 sentences.

6 students always cut up old cards.

Ask at the Bank

The Project: Create a poster about banking services
Materials: poster board, markers, brochures from local banks describing
banking services, and bank websites (if computers are available)

Why We Go to the Bank

Banking Services	Reasons to Use
ATM	to get money quickly

1. Work with 4–5 students. Introduce yourself.

2. Choose your job.

> **Leader:** Help your group work together.
> **Timekeeper:** Watch the time.
> **Recorder:** Write the team's ideas.
> **Reporter:** Tell the class about the project.
> **Supplier:** Get the supplies.

3. Brainstorm the answer to this question: What are some important banking services?

> **Timekeeper:** Give the team 5 minutes.
> **Leader:** Ask each person the question.
> **Recorder:** Write the name and answers for each team member.

4. Make the poster.

> **Supplier:** Get the supplies from your teacher.
> **Team:** Think of the most important banking services and reasons why you use them.
> Make the poster. Label the columns "Banking Services" and "Reasons to Use."
> Write down each banking service and the reason to use it.
> **Leader:** Help the team think of a title.
> **Recorder:** Write the title on the poster.

5. Show your project to your class.

> **Reporter:** Tell the class about the poster.
> *Checking and savings accounts are very important banking services.*

> **KEEP GOING!**
> Work in your team. Decide which banking service is the most important.
> Circle that service on your poster.

Picture Cards

1. Cut apart the picture cards. Use the word list to write the words on the back.

2. Work with a partner.

   Partner A: Show the picture card to your partner.

   Partner B: Say the words.

3. Change roles.

WORD LIST		
9.1 withdraw money	9.5 choose another item	9.9 compare prices
9.2 deposit money	9.6 get a refund	9.10 buy a gift
9.3 apply for a credit card	9.7 make an exchange	9.11 use a coupon
9.4 get change	9.8 return an item	9.12 get a discount

Grid Game

1. Cut apart the picture cards from page 104.

2. Work with a partner. Don't show your paper to your partner.

Partner A: Put a picture on a square on the grid. Use the picture and the location in the square to make a sentence. Tell your partner the sentence: *She used a coupon at Gina's Shop.*

Partner B: Listen to your partner. Put the picture on the correct square. Check what you hear: *Where?*

3. When your grids are full, look at them. Are they the same?
Yes: change roles. No: try again.

Gina's Shop	Home Fair	Big Buy
Sam's Supermarket	The General Store	the ATM
Greenville Bank	Phil's Pharmacy	Stuff for You
Smart Clothes	Diana's Discount Store	Books and More

Sentence Maker

1. Work with a group of 3 or 4 students. Cut apart the cards.
2. Choose a Recorder.
3. Use the word cards to make 10 different sentences or questions in 10 minutes.
   The Recorder writes the group's sentences and questions.

SHE	I	THEY	OPEN
OPENED	WENT	GO	WITHDRAW
DEPOSIT	GET	MONEY	ATM
CHECKING ACCOUNT	BANK	DID	AT
THE	TO	.	?

Unit 10 Steps to Citizenship

Vote for Me

1. Work with 3 classmates.

2. Label what you see in the picture.

3. Check your spelling in a dictionary.

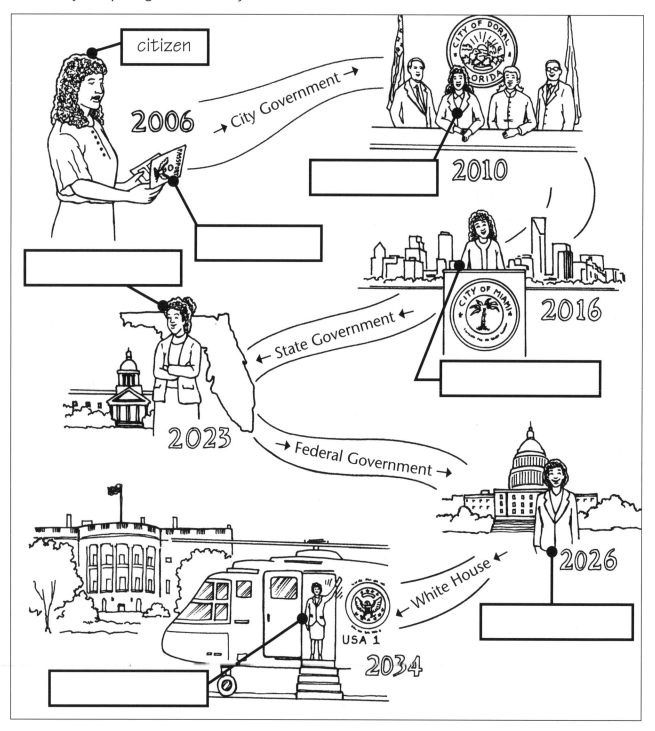

> ### KEEP GOING!
> Talk about your government officials. Do you know their names?

It's for the School

1. Work with a partner. Look at the pictures. Match the sentences to the pictures.

2. **Partner A:** Say the sentences.

   Partner B: Act out the sentences. Use actions and words.

3. Change roles.

____ Sell the cookies at school.

____ State the problem.

____ Take a vote.

1 Your school needs money. Go to a meeting.

____ List solutions.

____ Give the money to the school principal.

____ Go home and bake cookies.

____ Call the meeting to order.

KEEP GOING!

Work in a group. Take turns. Act out the sentences. Say what your classmate is doing.

Stay Safe

Partner A
• **Read a sentence to Partner B.** • **Answer Partner B's question.** • **Watch Partner B write.**
1. Mr. Perez must drive safely. 2. He must stop at a red light. 3. He must not go over the speed limit. 4. He must wear a seatbelt.
• **Listen to Partner B.** • **Check what you hear. Ask: *What must she do?*** • **Write the sentence.**
5.
6.
7.
8.

- FOLD HERE -

Partner B
• **Listen to Partner A.** • **Check what you hear. Ask: *What must he do?*** • **Write the sentence.**
1.
2.
3.
4.
• **Read a sentence to Partner A.** • **Answer Partner A's question.** • **Watch Partner A write.**
5. Mrs. Mason must obey the traffic laws. 6. She must wait for the walk signal. 7. She must not walk in the street. 8. She must always cross at the corner.

> **KEEP GOING!**
> Write 4 sentences about other things drivers and pedestrians must
> or must not do. Talk about your sentences with the class.
> *Drivers must not drive on the sidewalk.*

It Won't Happen Again!

1. Work with 2 classmates. Say all the lines in the script.

2. Choose your character.

3. Finish the conversation. Write more lines for each character.

4. Practice the lines.

5. Act out the role-play with your group.

Scene 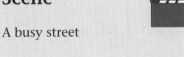	Characters	Props
A busy street	• Driver • Police Officer • Passenger	• Two chairs (front seat of car) • Traffic ticket book • Driver's license

The Script

Driver: Hello, Officer.

Police Officer: Hello. May I see your driver's license and registration?

Driver: Sure. Here it is.

Police Officer: Did you know you were speeding?

Passenger: No, he didn't, officer.

Driver: I thought the speed limit was 45 miles per hour.

Police Officer: Yes, it is, but you were going 60 miles per hour. That wasn't your only mistake.

KEEP GOING!

Watch your classmates' role-plays. Write the answers to these questions: What other mistakes did the driver make? Did the police officer give the driver a ticket?

The United States Government

1. Read the survey questions. Mark your answer with a check (✓).
2. Interview 3–9 classmates. Check your classmates' answers.

Can you name _____?	My Answers	My Classmates' Answers								
		1	2	3	4	5	6	7	8	9
the president										
the vice president										
the 3 branches of the government										
the number of justices on the Supreme Court										
the number of senators in the U.S. Senate										

3. Use the chart above to complete the bar graph.

Number of Classmates					
10					
9					
8					
7					
6					
5					
4					
3					
2					
1					
	knew the president's name	knew the vice president's name	knew the 3 branches of government	knew the number of justices on the Supreme Court	knew the number of U.S. senators

KEEP GOING!

Discuss this information with your class. Write 5 sentences.

Every student knows the names of the president and vice president.

Safety Signs

The Project: Create flash cards of rules for teachers, people on first dates, pet owners, parents, etc.

Materials: large blank index cards, markers, colored pencils, or crayons

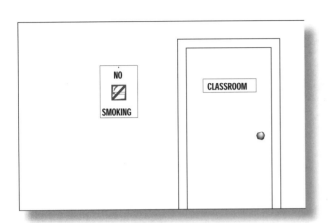
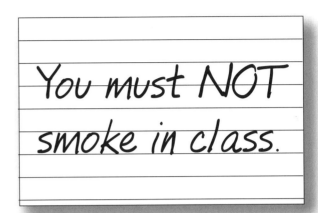

1. Work with 4–5 students. Introduce yourself.

2. Choose your job.

> **Leader:** Help your group work together.
> **Timekeeper:** Watch the time.
> **Recorder:** Write the team's ideas.
> **Reporter:** Tell the class about the project.
> **Supplier:** Get the supplies.

3. Choose a topic: rules for teachers, people on first dates, pet owners, parents, or other people. Brainstorm answers to this question: What are rules that you should follow as a _____ ?

> **Timekeeper:** Give the team 5 minutes.
> **Leader:** Help the team choose a topic. Then ask each person the question.
> **Recorder:** Write the name and answers for each team member.

4. Make the flash cards.

> **Supplier:** Get the supplies from your teacher.
> **Team:** Make a flash card for each rule. Draw a picture on one side of the flash card and write the rule on the other side.

5. Show your project to your class.

> **Reporter:** Show the class the pictures on your flash cards. Ask: *Which rule is this?* Listen to the guesses and then read the rule.

> **KEEP GOING!**
> Change flash cards with another group. Look at each card and guess the rule from the picture on the flash card. If you don't know, turn the card over for the answer.

Picture Cards

1. Cut apart the picture cards. Use the word list to write the words on the back.

2. Work with a partner.

    Partner A: Show the picture card to your partner.

    Partner B: Say the words.

3. Change roles.

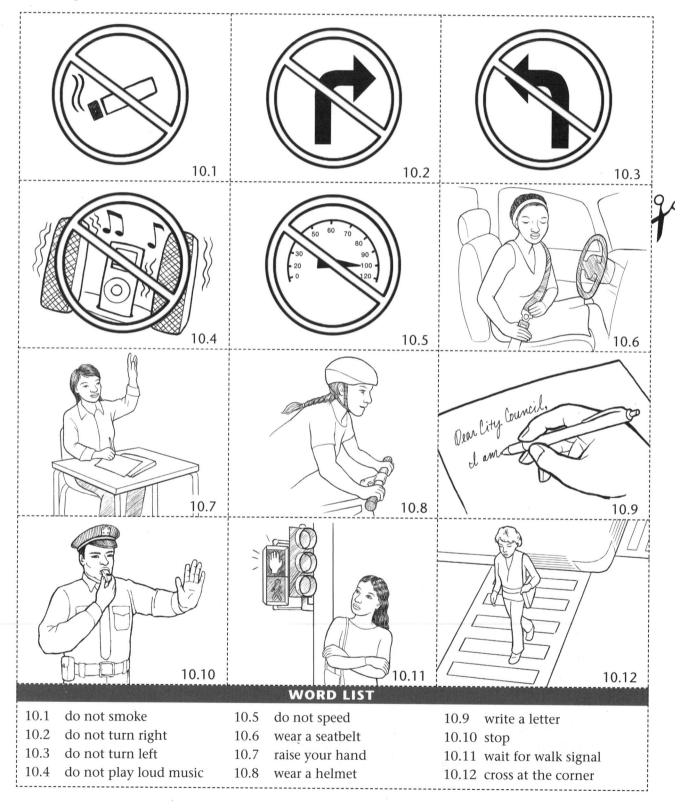

10.1 do not smoke	10.5 do not speed	10.9 write a letter
10.2 do not turn right	10.6 wear a seatbelt	10.10 stop
10.3 do not turn left	10.7 raise your hand	10.11 wait for walk signal
10.4 do not play loud music	10.8 wear a helmet	10.12 cross at the corner

WORD LIST

Grid Game

1. Cut apart the picture cards from page 114.

2. Work with a partner. Don't show your paper to your partner.

Partner A: Put a picture on a square on the grid. Use the picture and the subject in the square to make a sentence. Tell your partner the sentence: *You should not smoke.*

Partner B: Listen to your partner. Put the picture on the correct square.

Check what you hear: *Pardon me?*

3. When your grids are full, look at them. Are they the same?

Yes: change roles. No: try again.

you	I	we
they	Brenda	Emilia and Sharma
Tara	Mr. Jones	Mrs. Smith
Adam and Fernando	Tony	Barbara and Ana

Sentence Maker

1. Work with a group of 3 or 4 students. Cut apart the cards.
2. Choose a Recorder.
3. Use the word cards to make 10 different sentences or questions in 10 minutes.
   The Recorder writes the group's sentences and questions.

SHE	THEY	YOU	MUST
SHOULD	NOT	WEAR	HAVE
TAKE	SPEED	SEATBELT	REGISTRATION
DRIVER'S LICENSE	TEST	CITIZENSHIP	SMOKE
THE	A	.	?

Unit 11 Deal with Difficulties

Natural Disasters

1. Work with 3 classmates.

2. Label what you see in the picture.

3. Check your spelling in a dictionary.

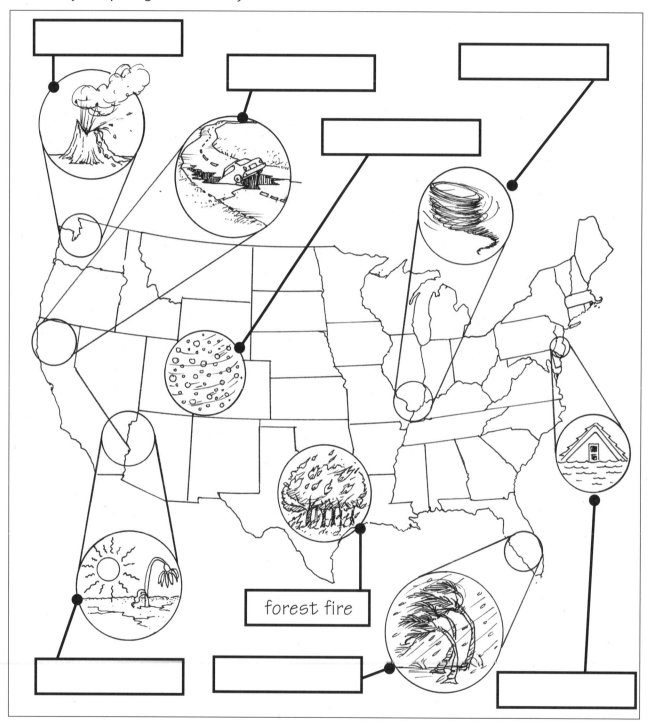

forest fire

KEEP GOING!
Talk about where natural disasters occur. What natural disasters occur in the Southwest?
In the Northeast?

George Has an Emergency!

1. Work with a partner. Look at the pictures. Match the sentences to the pictures.

2. Partner A: Say the sentences.

   Partner B: Act out the sentences. Use actions and words.

3. Change roles.

_____ Ask to use the telephone.

_____ Your phone isn't working. Run to your neighbor's house.

_____ Call 911.

_____ You're upset. Use the fire extinguisher.

_____ Look in the kitchen. Shout, "Fire!"

_____ Tell the operator about the fire.

_____ Bang on the door.

_1_ You're in the living room. You smell smoke.

KEEP GOING!

Work in a group. Take turns. Act out the sentences. Say what your classmate is doing.

He Usually Drives

Partner A
• **Read a sentence to Partner B.**   • **Answer Partner B's question.**   • **Watch Partner B write.**
1. How does Ramiro usually go to work?   2. He drives every day.   3. Last Friday, he didn't drive because it was raining.   4. He took the bus.
• **Listen to Partner B.**   • **Check what you hear. Ask: *What did you say?***   • **Write the sentence.**
5.
6.
7.
8.

- FOLD HERE -

Partner B
• **Listen to Partner A.**   • **Check what you hear. Ask: *What did you say?***   • **Write the sentence.**
1.
2.
3.
4.
• **Read a sentence to Partner A.**   • **Answer Partner A's question.**   • **Watch Partner A write.**
5. Does Ella often walk home from work?   6. No, she doesn't, but she walked home yesterday.   7. She wanted to get some exercise.   8. She usually exercises on the weekends.

KEEP GOING!

Write 4 sentences about different ways to get to work or school. How do you usually get to work or school? Talk about your sentences with the class.

I usually drive to work, but sometimes I walk.

A Robbery!

1. Work with 2 classmates. Say all the lines in the script.

2. Choose your character.

3. Finish the conversation. Write more lines for each character.

4. Practice the lines.

5. Act out the role-play with your group.

Scene	Characters	Props
At home	• 911 operator • Caller • Teenager	• Table • Two telephones

The Script

911 Operator: What's your emergency?

Caller: I need the police. I came home and my window was broken, and the door was open.

Teenager: I'm so upset!

911 Operator: What's your location?

Caller: I'm at home. My address is 342 Oakfield Road.

Teenager: Oh, no! Lots of stuff is missing!

Caller: Many items are missing.

911 Operator: What's missing?

KEEP GOING!

Watch your classmates' role-plays. Write the answers to these questions:
What's missing? What does the operator tell the caller to do?

The Same Thing Happened to Me

1. Read the survey questions. Mark your answer with a check (✓).

2. Interview 3–9 classmates. Check your classmates' answers.

Did you ever have a _____?	My Answers	My Classmates' Answers								
		1	2	3	4	5	6	7	8	9
bicycle stolen										
broken leg										
car accident										
fire at home										
flood at home										
robbery										

3. Use the chart above to complete the bar graph.

Number of Classmates						
10						
9						
8						
7						
6						
5						
4						
3						
2						
1						
	bicycle stolen	broken leg	car accident	fire at home	flood at home	robbery

KEEP GOING!

Share this information with your class. Write 5 sentences.
6 students had a broken leg.

Be Ready for Anything

The Project: Make a natural disaster flyer
Materials: blank paper, crayons, markers, Internet information on how
to prepare for natural disasters (if computer available)

Prepare for a Hurricane

What to do	What you need
Listen to weather reports.	Water
Put up hurricane shutters.	Canned food

---

1. Work with 4–5 students. Introduce yourself.

2. Choose your job.

> **Leader:** Help your group work together.
> **Timekeeper:** Watch the time.
> **Recorder:** Write the team's ideas.
> **Reporter:** Tell the class about the project.
> **Supplier:** Get the supplies.

3. Brainstorm answers to this question: What are some natural disasters?

> **Timekeeper:** Give the team 5 minutes.
> **Leader:** Ask each person the question.
> **Recorder:** Write the names and answers for each team member.

4. Make the flyer.

> **Supplier:** Get the supplies from your teacher.
> **Team:** Choose one natural disaster.
> • Write the information about this natural disaster on the flyer.
> • Make a list of items you need and how to prepare for this natural disaster.
> • Draw a picture of the natural disaster.
> **Leader:** Help the team think of a title.
> **Recorder:** Write the title on the flyer.

5. Show your project to your class.

> **Reporter:** Tell the class about the flyer.
> *These are the things you should do if there is a hurricane.*

KEEP GOING!
Make a natural disaster kit with items from the flyer. Place them in a small
box to use if there is a natural disaster.

Picture Cards

1. Cut apart the picture cards. Use the word list to write the words on the back.

2. Work with a partner.

    Partner A: Show the picture card to your partner.

    Partner B: Say the words.

3. Change roles.

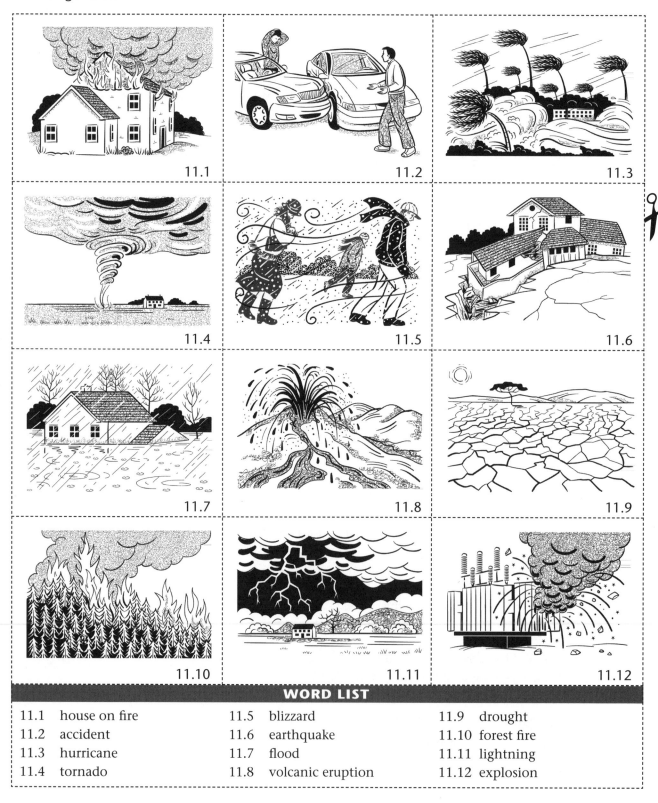

WORD LIST		
11.1 house on fire	11.5 blizzard	11.9 drought
11.2 accident	11.6 earthquake	11.10 forest fire
11.3 hurricane	11.7 flood	11.11 lightning
11.4 tornado	11.8 volcanic eruption	11.12 explosion

Grid Game

1. Cut apart the picture cards from page 124.

2. Work with a partner. Don't show your paper to your partner.
Partner A: Put a picture on a square on the grid. Use the picture and the location in the square to make a sentence. Tell your partner the sentence: *There was a drought in the Southwest.*
Partner B: Listen to your partner. Put the picture on the correct square. Check what you hear: *Where was it?*

3. When your grids are full, look at them. Are they the same?
Yes: change roles. No: try again.

Southwest	Southeast	Northwest
Northeast	Midwest	California
Washington State	New York	Texas
Florida	San Francisco	Arizona

Sentence Maker

1. Work with a group of 3 or 4 students. Cut apart the cards.

2. Choose a Recorder.

3. Use the word cards to make 10 different sentences or questions in 10 minutes.
The Recorder writes the group's sentences and questions.

SHE	HE	YOU	WHERE
WHEN	DID	WAS	WERE
DRIVE	DROVE	DRIVING	SCHOOL
ACCIDENT	HAD	HAVE	WORK
AN	TO	.	?

Unit 12 Take the Day Off

We Like to Be Outdoors

1. Sit with 3 classmates.

2. Work together. Label what you see in the picture.

3. Check your spelling in the dictionary.

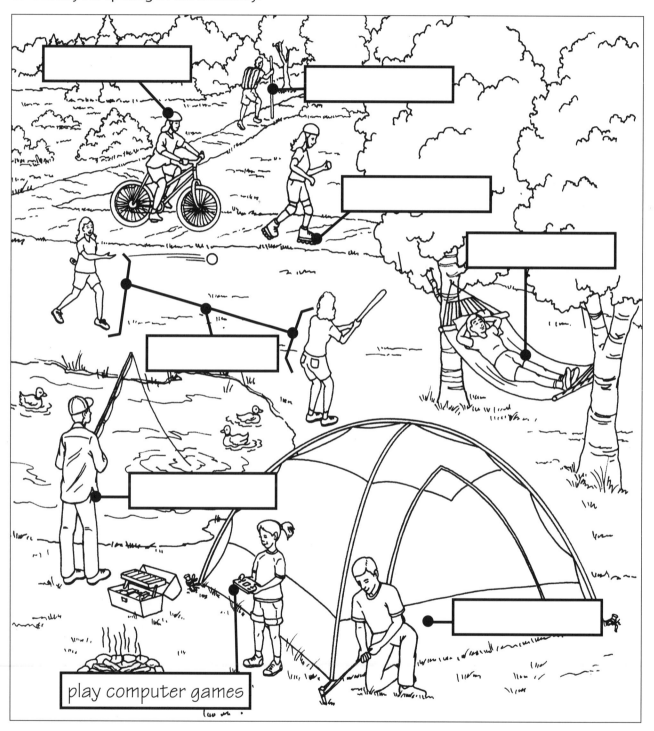

play computer games

KEEP GOING!

Talk about other kinds of recreation and entertainment. What do you like to do?

Camping Fun

1. Work with a partner. Look at the pictures. Match the sentences to the pictures.

2. **Partner A:** Say the sentences.

   Partner B: Act out the sentences. Use actions and words.

3. Change roles.

_____ Relax. Look at the stars.

_____ Get on your bike.
Bike to the lake.

_____ Oh no, the fish is gone!
Hike to the store.

_____ You're tired. Go to sleep.

_____ Go fishing. Catch a big fish.

_____ Build a fire.

_1_ You're camping. Set up your tent.

_____ Cook dinner.

KEEP GOING!
Work in a group. Take turns. Act out the sentences. Say what your classmate is doing.

Ted's List Is Better

Partner A
• **Read a sentence to Partner B.**   • **Answer Partner B's question.**   • **Watch Partner B write.**
1. According to Ted, the most expensive hotel is in Paris.   2. The most popular sport is soccer.   3. The most famous movie star is Grace Kelly.   4. The best list maker is Ted.
• **Listen to Partner B.**   • **Check what you hear. Ask:** *What does Ted say?*   • **Write the sentence.**
5.
6.
7.
8.

- - - - - - - - - - - - - - - - - - FOLD HERE - - - - - - - - - - - - - - - - - - -

Partner B
• **Listen to Partner A.**   • **Check what you hear. Ask:** *What does Min say?*   • **Write the sentence.**
1.
2.
3.
4.
• **Read a sentence to Partner A.**   • **Answer Partner A's question.**   • **Watch Partner A write.**
5. According to Min, the most expensive hotel is in Miami.   6. The most popular sport is softball.   7. The most famous movie star is Gary Cooper.   8. The worst list maker is Min.

KEEP GOING!

Write 4 sentences about the most, the worst, and the best. Make your own list about sports, people, and movies. Talk about your list with the class.
The best sport is biking.

Science Fiction Is the Best!

1. Work with 3 classmates. Say all the lines in the script.

2. Choose your character.

3. Finish the conversation. Write more lines for each character.

4. Practice the lines.

5. Act out the role-play with your group.

Scene	Characters	Props
A restaurant	• Friend 1 • Friend 2 • Friend 3 • Waiter	• Table • Newspaper • Coffee cups

The Script

Friend 1: Did you see the horror movie on TV last night?

Friend 2: I really don't like horror movies. I was watching a mystery movie.

Friend 3: I think romantic movies are more interesting.

Friend 2: Romantic movies are boring!

Waiter: Are you ready to order?

Friend 3: Let's ask the waiter.

Friend 2: What kind of movies do you like?

KEEP GOING!

Watch your classmates' role-plays. Write the answers to these questions: What kind of movies does the waiter like? What kind of movies does everyone like to watch?

What Do You Like to Watch?

1. Read the survey questions and mark your answer with a check (✓).

2. Interview 3–9 classmates. Check your classmates' answers.

What do you watch on TV?	My Answers	My Classmates' Answers								
		1	2	3	4	5	6	7	8	9
movies										
sports										
science fiction shows										
educational shows										
mystery shows										
quiz shows										

3. Use the chart above to complete the bar graph.

Number of Classmates						
10						
9						
8						
7						
6						
5						
4						
3						
2						
1						
	movies	sports	science fiction shows	educational shows	mystery shows	quiz shows

KEEP GOING!

Discuss this information with your class. What do your classmates watch on TV? Write 5 sentences.

3 students watch science fiction shows.

Local Sights

The Project: Create a poster about a famous or interesting place in your area
Materials: poster board, markers, colored pencils, glue
Resources: library books, the phone book's yellow pages, brochures
for local sights, and information from the Internet

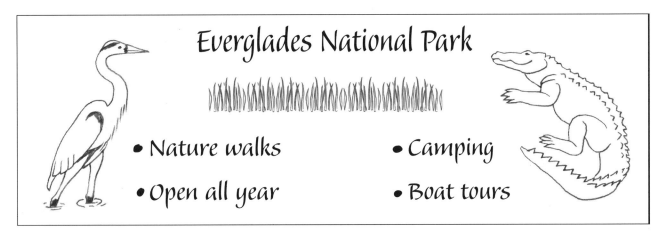

1. Work with 4–5 students. Introduce yourself.

2. Choose your job.

> **Leader:** Help your group work together.
> **Timekeeper:** Watch the time.
> **Recorder:** Write the team's ideas.
> **Reporter:** Tell the class about the project.
> **Supplier:** Get the supplies.

3. Brainstorm answers to this question: What are some famous or interesting
places in your area?

> **Timekeeper:** Give the team 5 minutes.
> **Leader:** Ask each person the question.
> **Recorder:** Write the names and answers for each team member.

4. Make the poster.

> **Supplier:** Get the supplies from your teacher.
> **Team:** Choose one sight. Get information about your place to put on the poster.
> Find out when it opens and when it closes, the address, and what you will see
> and what you can do there.

5. Show your project to the class.

> **Reporter:** Tell the class about the poster.
> *Our place is Everglades National Park. It is open from 9:00 a.m. to 5:00 p.m. every day.*

> **KEEP GOING!**
> Share your posters with other classes. Ask permission to talk about your local sights.

Picture Cards

1. Cut apart the picture cards. Use the word list to write the words on the back.

2. Work with a partner.

   Partner A: Show the picture card to your partner.

   Partner B: Say the words.

3. Change roles.

12.1	12.2	12.3
12.4	12.5	12.6
12.7	12.8	12.9
12.10	12.11	12.12

WORD LIST

12.1 playing football	12.5 going to the beach	12.9 going skating
12.2 playing softball	12.6 going hiking	12.10 watching TV
12.3 playing basketball	12.7 going biking	12.11 going to a museum
12.4 watching movies	12.8 going jogging	12.12 eating out

Grid Game

1. Cut apart the picture cards from page 134.

2. Work with a partner. Don't show your paper to your partner.

Partner A: Put a picture on a square on the grid. Use the picture and the phrase in the square to make a sentence. Tell your partner the sentence: *Playing football is the most exciting activity.*

Partner B: Listen to your partner. Put the picture on the correct square. Check what you hear: *What do you think?*

3. When your grids are full, look at them. Are they the same? Yes: change roles. No: try again.

the most interesting	the scariest	the most fantastic
the most exciting	the worst	the most boring
the healthiest	the most relaxing	the most dangerous
the most expensive	the cheapest	the best

Sentence Maker

1. Work with a group of 3 or 4 students. Cut apart the cards.

2. Choose a Recorder.

3. Use the word cards to make 10 different sentences or questions in 10 minutes.
The Recorder writes the group's sentences and questions.

IT	THEY	HE	IS
ARE	GOING	MOST	MORE
INTERESTING	BORING	MOVIES	SOCCER
THAN	SPORT	MYSTERY	ROMANTIC
TO	THE	.	?